DON'T LEAP
W I T H   T H E
SHEEP

DON'T LEAP
WITH THE
SHEEP

AND OTHER SCRIPTURAL

STRATEGIES FOR AVOIDING

SATAN'S SNARES

S. MICHAEL WILCOX

DESERET
BOOK

SALT LAKE CITY, UTAH

Library of Congress Cataloging-in-Publication Data

Wilcox, S. Michael.
    Don't leap with the sheep : and other scriptural strategies for avoiding Satan's snares / S. Michael Wilcox.
        p.   cm.
    Includes bibliographical references and index.
    ISBN 1-57008-719-9 (alk. paper)
    1. Spiritual warfare. 2. Church of Jesus Christ of Latter-day Saints—Doctrines.
3. Mormon Church—Doctrines.   I. Title.
BT975 .W52 2001
248.4'89332—dc21   2001004410

Printed in the United States of America   72082-6854
Publishers Press, Salt Lake City, UT

10   9   8   7   6   5   4   3   2   1

CONTENTS

CLEARING THE MISTS

Only one man was never blinded by the mists of the adversary, and that was the Lord Jesus Christ. "[He] was in all points tempted like as we are," wrote Paul, "yet without sin." (Hebrews 4:15.) All the rest of us have had our judgment dimmed by the darkness spread by the tempter. Even one as righteous as Nephi cried out in the anguish of his soul, "O wretched man that I am! . . . I am encompassed about, because of the temptations and the sins which do so easily beset me. And when I desire to rejoice, my heart groaneth because of my sins." (2 Nephi 4:17–19.)

When Nephi wrote that expression, he added an eloquent prayer beseeching the Lord to help him resist every effort to divert him from the true purposes of life: "Wilt thou make me that I may shake at the appearance of sin? May the gates of hell be shut continually before me, because that my heart is broken and my spirit is contrite! O Lord, wilt thou not shut the gates of thy righteousness before me, that I may walk in the path of the low valley, that I may be strict in the plain road! O Lord, wilt thou encircle me around in the robe of thy righteousness! . . . Wilt thou make my path straight before me! Wilt thou not place a stumbling block in my way—but . . . clear my way before me." (2 Nephi 4:31–33.)

If even the most righteous felt a need to pray this way, what does that teach the rest of us? We may use other words, but the emotion and the earnestness must be the same. This is particularly true since we live in a world where "the powers of darkness prevail upon the earth, among the children of men." (D&C 38:11.) It is also true in light of the eternal consequences of this life, which are too important for us to fail.

ENTHRONED IN GLORY

Brigham Young described the importance of life by saying, "Mankind are organized of element designed to endure to all eternity. . . . It is brought together, organized, and capacitated to receive knowledge and intelligence, to be enthroned in glory, to be made angels, Gods—beings who will hold control over the elements, and have power by their word to command the creation and redemption of worlds, or to extinguish suns by their breath, and disorganize worlds, hurling them back into their chaotic state. This is what you and I are created for." (*Journal of Discourses*, 26 vols. [London: Latter-day Saints' Book Depot, 1854–86], 3:356.)

Since the Lord knew we would live in a mortal world where the mists of darkness would be so dominant, and since he understands the eternal consequences of life, it would be surprising indeed if he did not include in his great plan of happiness the means necessary for his children to see through the mists and obtain the celestial prize. This would, of necessity, be a central theme in all his communications with his children on the earth.

THE BEST BOOKS

My grandfather was a great hero to me as I grew up. He allowed me to work with him and would discuss scripture stories with me as though I were an equal even when I was just a boy. I remember vividly the image of my grandpa sitting in his big green rocking chair with the Bible open on his lap. I can smell the leather and feel the tiny ripples and soft creases of the binding. I can hear the sound the pages made as he turned them. There is no sound equal to that sacred rustle of the thin leaves of what God himself called "the best books." I believe that the Lord smiles when he hears that sound ascending from our homes. Few memories of my childhood bring a greater warmth of security than this one of my grandfather. I believe that the Lord anchored that memory in my mind as a future guide.

When the potential to receive "a far more, and an exceeding, and an eternal weight of glory" (D&C 132:16) rests upon us; when we view our own frailness in facing the opposition spoken of by Nephi; when we feel compelled to pray, "Father in Heaven, don't let us fail! Clear the mists of darkness from before us that we may partake of the fruit of the tree of life!" there is calm assurance available. If we listen carefully, we will hear the Lord answer, "I will! I can! I have!" When these times come in my own life, into my mind a memory distills. I see the familiar face of my grandfather, feel the soft leather binding of his scriptures, and hear again that holy rustle of pages turning through his fingers. The individual stories recorded on those sacred leaves come to mind, and the mists never fail to clear.

CHAPTER ONE

THE FINAL BATTLE

The first general conference session I ever attended made a deep impression on me. I was seventeen and had waited in line outside the Tabernacle several hours to obtain a seat in the gallery. President Hugh B. Brown was a counselor in the First Presidency at the time. It was the middle of the '60s, and the moral climate of America was in decline. At the end of his address, President Brown spoke directly to the young men in the audience, and his words went to the center of my soul:

"I hope that every young man under the sound of my voice will resolve tonight, 'I'm going to keep myself clean. I'm going to serve the Lord. I am going to prepare every way I can for future service, because I want to be prepared when *the final battle shall come.*' And some of you young men are going to engage in that battle. Some of you are going to engage in the final testing time, which is coming and is closer to us than we know. . . .

"There is a spirit hovering over this group and reaching out to the various groups who are listening in. It is the Spirit of the Holy Ghost, calling upon all men who have been baptized into the Church and have received some order of priesthood to stand up and be counted, for the time will come when those who are not for him will be found to be against him. I urge all of us to set our houses in order, to set our lives in order, to be prepared for that which lies ahead."

When President Brown spoke of the final battle, I could almost see the forces of good and the forces of evil lined up against each other. I felt a sense of anxiety, wondering if I would be prepared enough to be part of the final victory that would surely follow this prophetic battle. President Brown then paused for a few moments, turned his head upward, and began to pray for all the young men in the Church. He seemed to be talking to the Lord as if standing in front of Him, and the Tabernacle was filled with an intensity of the Spirit I had never experienced before.

"O Father, bless these young men, and these older ones. Let thy Spirit guide them. May it hover over them, shield and protect them against the wiles of the adversary. We realize, O Father, that they are fighting not against flesh and blood alone. They are fighting against enemies in high places. They are fighting against empires. They are fighting against organized sin, organized rebellion. They are fighting against riots and all manner of disobedience and lawlessness.

"O Father, help these young men who are listening tonight, when they go home to get on their knees and commit themselves to thee; and then they may know and I promise them in thy name that they will know, that with thy help they need not fear the future." (In Conference Report, October 1967, pp. 115–17.)

I did go home and get on my knees, as President Brown had urged us. His promise was true. I knew in that moment that there was no need to fear but just to prepare. We sing from time to time the words, "We are all enlisted till the conflict is o'er; Happy are we! Happy are we! Soldiers in the army, there's a bright crown in store; We shall win and wear it by and by." (*Hymns*, no. 250.) Soon after this life-changing session of general conference, I began to understand how the Lord had been preparing his people to face the final battle. Because of the Lord's wisdom in that preparation, we may indeed sing, "Happy are we!"

THE BATTLE PLANS

During a critical juncture of the American Civil War, Robert E. Lee, eager to strike a crippling blow at the Union forces, marched into Maryland. His strategy was set and his orders issued. Order 191 described in detail Lee's decision to split his army as they marched north. Unfortunately for General Lee, one of his officers lost the order, and it was found by two Union soldiers, who immediately took it to General George McClellan, head of the Union forces.

McClellan now knew the exact position of his enemy and planned his defense and attack accordingly. When handed the lost orders, McClellan waved them before the eyes of another Union general and triumphantly said, "Here is a paper with which, if I cannot whip Bobby Lee, I will be willing to go home." The subsequent battle of Antietam turned back the Southern advance, kept the European nations from recognizing the Confederacy, and became one of the chief turning points in a devastating war.

How advantageous it is to know the battle plans of the enemy and be allowed to respond accordingly! On earth we are engaged in the most serious of conflicts—the battle for the souls of our Father in Heaven's children: "[Satan] maketh war with the saints of God, and encompasseth them round about." (D&C 76:29.) There are far too many casualties.

We may be encouraged in the knowledge that one of the first prophecies recorded in the history of this earth concerned the outcome of this great spiritual battle. The Lord simply but firmly indicated that Lucifer would be crushed. The outcome is certain; the final victory has already been proclaimed. Before that final triumph, however, each of us must win our personal battles. We must stand firm in defending our part of the line. It will not be a long war, but it will be intense. John wrote, "The devil is come down unto you, having great wrath, because he knoweth that he hath *but a short time*." (Revelation 12:12. Emphasis has been added here and in other scriptures in this book.) And Nephi prophesied that the devil shall "*rage* in the hearts of the children of men." (2 Nephi 28:20.)

During that "short time" of "rage" we must be prepared, and the Lord has given us the very battle plans of the adversary to help us in our preparation. He has also armed us with his own defense and plan of attack to counter those of the tempter. Satan's plans and our defense against them are recorded in detail in the scriptures. Indeed, one of the major purposes of holy writ is to detail the parameters of the battle. The words of the Lord are "quick and powerful, sharper than a two-edged sword," which can "divide asunder all the cunning and the snares and the wiles of the devil." (D&C 6:2; Helaman 3:29.) With the scriptures in hand we may say as did George McClellan, "Here is a [book] with which, if I cannot whip [the devil], I will be willing to go home."

"IT IS WRITTEN"

As in every aspect of life, the Savior is our example. He is our general and leads our attack. Early in the gospels that record His life, we are invited to watch Him do battle with the arch tempter. When Jesus was tempted to gratify His physical demands, He replied, "*It is written,* Man shall not live by bread alone, but by every word that proceedeth out of the mouth of God." (Matthew 4:4.) Quoting Moses and remembering the story of manna in the wilderness, he drew strength to dismiss the adversary's suggestion.

He repelled Satan's suggestion that He put God to the test

by leaping from the pinnacle of the temple with the words, "*It is written again*, Thou shalt not tempt the Lord thy God." (Matthew 4:7.) Relying on the words of Moses while reflecting on the story of the water from the rock, Jesus recognized Lucifer's strategy and repulsed it.

A third time the devil attacked. While Christ viewed all the kingdoms of the world and their glory, the tempting voice murmured, "All these things will I give thee, if thou wilt . . . worship me." Again, drawing upon His vast reservoir of knowledge of the Old Testament, Jesus countered, "Get thee hence, Satan: for *it is written*, Thou shalt worship the Lord thy God, and him only shalt thou serve." (Matthew 4:9–10.)

The common denominator in each of the three examples is the phrase *It is written*. From years of previous study, the Savior was armed and ready for whatever suggestion the evil one had to offer. We must do as He did. When the arch deceiver comes with his delusive mists, it is often too late for preparation. We must learn to wield the sword of the scriptures before he advances. Important counsel the Lord gave to those of us who dwell on earth just prior to His Second Coming was, "Whoso *treasureth* up my word, shall not be deceived." (Joseph Smith—Matthew, 1:37.)

Throughout my life, while facing, as we all do, various mists of temptation from the adversary, I have collected a number of "it is written" stories and truths that have been effective in unmasking the guile of our common enemy. I have tried to reduce these defenses to simple, easy-to-remember phrases or questions that bring to my mind the full account and message of the scriptural example. I repeat them to myself from time to time: The safest place in the world is the back of a horse! Stay away from Caiaphas' palace! Wave your title of liberty! Fight the lion and the bear first! Don't lick grass! Talk with the donkey! Don't jump off the pinnacle! Am I crowning a king? Will I shed Esau tears? Am I making bricks without straw? Is it wall-watching or grape-gathering? Beware of Noah blindness! You can't catch a snipe! These and many others have saved me countless times from the obscuring mists of him who was a liar from the beginning. In the following pages, I will share some of these with you, in the hope that they will prove useful in the great battle in which we are all engaged.

FIGHT IN FAMILY FORMATION

There is one thing we can be sure of in our battles: The Lord anticipates that we will fight in *family formation*. The family is the primary striking unit in the Lord's army. It is in the family where we can most effectively learn how to wield the sword of the scriptures. I loved to play chess as a boy, and the knight was my favorite piece. Because of this I left my queen standing idly by while I maneuvered my two knights all over the board. I lost many games this way until I learned that the queen was the most effective piece on the board. She then became my principal fighter while the other pieces supported her in this role. If we are not careful, we may repeat in life my youthful mistake. We may have a favorite organization or activity and spend the majority of our time or effort in that area. The Church itself is not the strongest piece on the board. Rather, the family is the queen. It must be our principal fighter. All other organizations in life are in a supporting role.

One of my favorite parables of Jesus covers only one verse, but I have thought of it often as I have taught the scriptures over the years: "Every scribe which is instructed unto the kingdom of heaven is like unto a man that is an householder, which bringeth forth out of his treasure things new and old." (Matthew 13:52.) The scriptures are our treasure. Some stories we return to again and again—like old friends. They strengthen us with their familiar power. But if we continue to search, we will always find new gems of wisdom to inspire and lead us. I invite you to come with me as we pull from the treasure chest those old and new jewels, radiant with divine light, that have cleared and will continue to clear the mists of darkness in our lives.

CHAPTER TWO

WHAT THE
MISTS HIDE

One of the first truths the Lord revealed about "the father of all lies" was his purpose "to deceive and to *blind* men." (Moses 4:4.) There must, therefore, be certain things he does not wish us to see. Blinding us to these things appears to be one of his main strategies.

In Lehi's dream this desire to blind is represented by "a mist of darkness; yea, even an exceedingly great mist of darkness." (1 Nephi 8:23.) There are three things in Lehi's dream that are obscured by the mist and that correspond to the reality of our mortal lives. Satan does not want us to see the tree of life, which we are told symbolizes the love of God. He does not want us to perceive the rod of iron, or the word of God, which will keep us on the path when the tree is lost from our view. He is also desirous that we know nothing of the filthy river or the consequences of misery, both temporal and eternal, which come for those who leave the path and their pursuit of the happiness that comes in partaking of the tree. Simply put, the mists hide the sources of both happiness and misery and the necessary thing that will help us obtain the one while avoiding the other.

The only major symbol in Lehi's dream that Lucifer does not want to hide is the spacious building, which symbolizes pride and the vain things of the world. Through the mists he whispers, "There is no loving God! There is no eternal truth! There are no consequences for sin! The only reality is the pleasures and treasures of the world, which are found in the building 'high above the earth.' (1 Nephi 8:26.)"

DESIRABLE ABOVE ALL

One of the most crucial things we must remember if we are to pass through the mists safely is the nature of the tree as it is described throughout the Book of Mormon. Seven adjectives detail the value of the tree. If we read closely, we will notice that all seven words are used with a comparative phrase. The words are *sweet, white, desirable, beautiful, precious, joyous,* and *pure.* Notice, however, the full phrases that contain these adjectives:

1. "Most sweet, *above all* that I ever before tasted."

2. "The fruit thereof was white, *to exceed all* the whiteness that I had ever seen."

3. "I knew that it was desirable *above all other* fruit." (1 Nephi 8:11–12.)

4. "The beauty thereof was *far beyond, yea, exceeding of all beauty.*"

5. "Thou hast shown unto me the tree which is precious *above all.*"

6. "Yea, and *the most* joyous to the soul." (1 Nephi 11:8–9, 23.)

7. "Pure *above all* that is pure." (Alma 32:42.)

There simply isn't anything the world can offer in the building to compare with what the Lord offers. The multitudes Lehi saw wandering in the mists were looking for the fulfillment that only the tree can offer. It is no wonder the tempter wishes to hide the fruit "desirable to make one happy" (1 Nephi 8:10), "for he seeketh that all men might be miserable like unto himself." (2 Nephi 2:27.)

BORN WITH THE FRUIT IN OUR HANDS!

A close friend I have honored since my early youth once told me of leaving the rod and the tree to visit the spacious building many years ago. My friend was not gone long before returning, but he knew enough of both worlds to teach me a powerful lesson. "There is nothing in the building you want!" my friend often reminded me. "You already have the best there is in the world! You don't have to search for it. Don't be deceived as I was." These words were always spoken with great earnestness.

Perhaps the most powerful, mist-clearing truth is the assurance that we already have the most desirable thing in life. We don't have to wander in a vain pursuit of happiness. Many of us were born with the fruit in our hands. We sometimes hear the expression "How sweet it is!" This is usually spoken in the context of some worldly pursuit or pleasure. But we have that which is *sweet* above all things. As Alma testified, "It beginneth to be delicious to me." (Alma 32:28.) Nothing in life will give us more *joy* than that which we now possess. There simply isn't anything more *precious* we can obtain. Our eyes have already looked upon the greatest *beauty*.

BLINDED EYES AND HARDENED HEARTS

The tree offers us an invitation to partake of God's love. Its fruits are the countless ways that love is manifested, especially through the Savior's life, ministry, and atoning sacrifice. In the dream, the mists are designed to cause us to doubt God's love, to be blinded to His compassion. The temptations the mist represents are, therefore, conceived to turn us away from God so that we no longer believe He is a God of love who cares about each individual child. The angel revealed to Nephi that the mists also "hardeneth the hearts" of those who are lost in their darkness. Often the result of losing sight of God's love is a hardness that leads people "away into broad roads, that they perish and are lost." (1 Nephi 12:17.)

My best friend as a teenager was lost in such a mist during his experiences in Vietnam. He returned home bitter and angry against a God he no longer believed in. "If God exists," he told me, "he is not the God my Primary teacher told me about. I learned the truth in Vietnam. The truth is not prayer, because he never answered any of mine. He didn't care about anyone in Vietnam. The truth is just staying alive—making sure the enemy got the bullet instead of you. When I learned that, the killing didn't bother me anymore." Throughout the history of the world, the suffering caused by hate and war has blinded many eyes and hardened many hearts.

I am aware of a sister who became bitter after a lifetime of Church activity because her husband died a long, slow, painful death of cancer. This trial became her mist, removing from her sight the loving God she had served for so many years. In spite of prayers, fasts, and blessings, healing would not come. Then the prayers changed to a request that a final release from life would come quickly, but he lingered in pain. "Why would God treat us this way?" she asked. "Is this the reward we get for obedience and service?" Severe trials can numb our feelings of affection and trust in a Father in Heaven we believe controls all things. "Why will He not help us?" we may ask. "He must not care."

This was Job's dilemma when faced with the senseless evil that stripped him of every source of happiness. "Your children will love you only when all is well in their lives," Satan insisted. Yet from the ash heap of his agonies, Job still believed in a God of goodness and threw Satan's challenge back at him. He refused to let the mists of his own misery blind him to the loving God in whom he had always believed. His example is inspiring and instructive but hard to duplicate.

Sometimes guilt can be an effective mist that denies us the

needed taste of the fruit of the tree. "How can God still love me after what I have done?" we ask. "What hope for eternal happiness can I now have?" If this line of reasoning continues, it can lead us to let go of the rod, drop the fruit, and spend a life in the great and spacious building or wandering the "strange roads" and "forbidden paths," desperately searching for a substitute happiness to replace the one created by the gospel.

Even those who have trusted in the Atonement and received forgiveness may from time to time feel again the taint of unworthiness and wonder how God views them. They may have trouble forgiving themselves. In spite of all assurances to the contrary, the lingering mist of guilts long past may forever prevent them from seeing the details of God's mercy clearly. We must remember that Jesus said, "Go in peace," not in perpetual remorse over past transgressions.

There are a hundred and one ways in which we may fail to see the fruits of a loving God. When these times come, it is critical that we understand them for what they are and then grasp the iron rod more tightly by turning to the truths of the scriptures. In the light contained therein, we will feel the love of a Father in Heaven and His chosen Savior as it flows from a pure source.

As we will see in the coming chapters, almost every temptation of life is designed to accomplish three basic things: 1. Prevent our tasting or fully understanding the fruits of God's love. 2. Keep us from holding onto divine, eternal, and unchanging truth. 3. Hide from view or temporarily deny the natural consequences and misery that follow those who leave the strait and narrow path. The whole Book of Mormon and, indeed, all scripture can be read in light of this introductory vision of Father Lehi. Page after page and story after story assure us of a loving Father in Heaven and Savior, unfolding the life-changing truths of eternity and warning us plainly and powerfully of the eventual destiny of those who break our Father in Heaven's eternal laws.

CHAPTER THREE

THE FIRST
TEMPTATION

My senior year in high school, I enrolled in a karate class to learn the art of self-defense. We were taught many rules and strategies. One of the foremost was, "Use your best attack first." The idea behind this philosophy was to deliver the winning blow at the start of the conflict. If you did not succeed in ending the struggle, you might unnerve your opponent and keep him forever on the defensive. With this in mind, it is interesting to see which of the many mists, snares, and flaxen cords at the adversary's disposal he first used on mankind. It was equally interesting to me to discover what defense the Lord suggests we use against Satan's first temptation.

The Lord gave the defense before Lucifer even came with his tempting suggestion. In the Garden of Eden the Lord explained to Adam and Eve the basic rule of the garden: "Of *every* tree of the garden *thou mayest freely eat,* but of the tree of the knowledge of good and evil, thou shalt not eat of it, nevertheless, thou mayest choose for thyself, for it is given unto thee; but, remember that I forbid it, for in the day thou eatest thereof thou shalt surely die." (Moses 3:16–17.)

Notice that the Lord started his commandment in a positive manner. Adam and Eve could eat from dozens of trees. Only one was forbidden, and for good reason. The key word in the Lord's instructions is *every*. In light of the many trees they could partake of, one single tree that was forbidden did not seem so restrictive. This attitude is a great key to life and one of the most effective tools the Lord has provided to clear the mists we will surely encounter. Our Father in Heaven would have us live in a manner that constantly focuses our attention on the things we have and the things we are allowed, even encouraged, to do. If our view of life reflects this philosophy, we will live in gratitude and humility.

After this great counsel, the Lord left Adam and Eve to care for the garden. The tempter then entered the scene and suggested just the opposite approach to life. His first words to Eve reflect his desire to cast a mist over all the good things we can freely enjoy and focus our attention on the things that are forbidden: "Yea, hath God said—Ye shall *not* eat of *every tree* of the garden?" (Moses 4:7.) His words were almost the same as the Lord's. However, when he used the word *every*, he wanted Eve to concentrate only on the tree that had been forbidden. Lucifer desires us to focus on the things we do not have and cannot do. If our view of life reflects Lucifer's philosophy, we will be frustrated, angry, rebellious, and resentful most of our lives.

IS FREEDOM THE ONLY VIRTUE?

Inherent in Lucifer's words was the suggestion that Eve was not totally free. Something desirable was being denied her. The first temptation, in its broadest terms, is the suggestion that rules, commandments, policies, counsels, honor codes, laws, and so on are a limit to our freedom and that we therefore have a right to rebel against them. This temptation is especially useful in diluting the words of the prophets. Since the war in heaven was fought over the issue of moral agency, we can almost hear an angry Satan saying to the forces that expelled him, "You want to allow them freedom. I am going to suggest to them that all they *have* is freedom. They have no responsibilities, no restrictions—just pure, unopposed liberty. I will lead them to believe they have nothing but rights." The mist of the first temptation leads us to believe that commandments and rules are a form of bondage. It is easy to see Satan's ironic twist. He promises liberty while taking us captive through our own rebellious actions, but those actions are most often taken in the name of freedom.

It is not hard to decipher this as one of the great mists in the arsenal of Lucifer. He used it on Eve, and he continues to use it effectively today. We hear a constant chorus of voices justifying some of the worst sins of mankind, all in the name of rights and freedom. To a greater or lesser extent we have probably all been deceived by this mist. Elder Boyd K. Packer described the first temptation in this way:

"While we pass laws to reduce pollution of the earth, any proposal to protect the moral and spiritual environment is shouted down and marched against as infringing upon liberty, agency, freedom, the right to choose. . . . Those determined to transgress see any regulation of their life-style as interfering with their agency and seek to have their actions condoned by making them legal." (*Ensign*, May 1992, p. 66.)

I used to keep a "first temptation" file containing letters to the editor that I obtained from a number of different sources, including the *Daily Universe* at Brigham Young University. I often discussed them with my students. Someone was always chafing over one of the restrictions in the honor code. Students complained because they could not wear shorts or could not grow a beard. Some were angry over the requirement of ecclesiastical endorsement and required church attendance. Some letters were written by faculty members nervous over publication limitations. These decried the demon of censorship. Was not a university a place of open examination where every idea should be freely studied and published?

On a wider, national front, the letters and articles championed everything from pornography, free love, and abortion on demand to forcing the Boy Scouts to change their foundational philosophy and accept gay Scoutmasters. All these issues were presented in the sacrosanct name of liberty and freedom. The great irony is that those proposing such justifications feel they have taken the higher moral ground, for in their eyes freedom is the all-encompassing virtue.

YOKED AND BOUND

Korihor is a great example of how the first temptation can be used with great sophistication. He was laboring hard to destroy the commandments of Alma and the other church leaders. Notice the key first-temptation words in the following phrases: "O ye that are *bound down* under a foolish and vain hope, why do ye *yoke* yourselves with such foolish things? . . . I do not teach this people to *bind* themselves down under the foolish ordinances and performances which are laid down by ancient priests, to *usurp power and authority over them, to keep them in ignorance, that they may not lift up their heads.* . . . Ye say that this people is a *free people.* Behold, I say they are *in bondage.* . . . Ye keep them down, even as it were in *bondage,* . . . that they durst not look up with boldness, and that they durst not *enjoy their rights and privileges.*" (Alma 30:13, 23, 24, 27.)

The earliest introduction to the first temptation often comes when youth begin to challenge the authority of their parents. It is natural as we develop to want to strike out on our own, to think for ourselves. This is an important stage of growth, but it is also a dangerous stage because of the immaturity of the teenage years. Youth are especially vulnerable to first-temptation thinking. They may reject the fruit of nourishing trees simply because it belongs to another generation. In their search for their own fruit, the mist may descend, blinding them to goodness while directing their attention to forbidden things. Parental rules are then seen as attempts to maintain control. Parents must be wise in helping their children gain the maturity to make correct choices with ever-increasing control over their own lives. Wise parents, like our Father in Heaven in the Garden of Eden, will constantly point out to children the many things they are free to do and have, thus focusing their attention on the good as did God.

CLEARING THE MIST

Eve teaches us a masterful way of clearing the mists created by the first temptation. When Lucifer suggested to her that she was limited in her choices by the commandment of the Lord, she countered with her freedom to partake of so many other trees: "We may eat of the fruit of the trees of the garden." (Moses 4:8.) She then explained why she should not partake of the forbidden fruit: "God hath said—Ye shall not eat of it, neither shall ye touch it, lest ye die." (Moses 4:9.) Eve trusted the Lord's interdiction. The commandment was for her welfare. God loved her and had given the commandment to protect her. If we believe that the commandments are the loving arms of a protective Father in Heaven reaching out to us, we will have little difficulty in obeying them. However, if we feel they are barbed-wire fences designed to withhold pleasures and desirable experiences, we will rebel.

The necessity of thinking of the commandments as Eve did became crystal clear to me one Sunday evening right after President Ezra Taft Benson had delivered his talk on the importance of mothers being in the home. I was serving as a bishop at the time and had two conversations with two mothers relative to his counsel. One mother felt that the counsel was a continuation of the Brethren's determination to limit a woman's full opportunities. The other believed that the counsel was delivered for her own fulfillment and the happiness of her family. One continued to work outside the home, feeling justified in her decision: "Times have changed. This is not the '50s." She felt the counsel would limit her potential and the lifestyle a second income would provide. The other sought for ways to develop her talents in a home setting. She focused on what she could do within the boundaries of the prophet's counsel.

Youth can be taught to see these different attitudes and their consequences. There is a great difference in the responses teenagers will give about not dating before sixteen if they understand that the counsel is not given to delay their enjoyment of social activities but to protect them from situations they may not have the maturity to control. They are much more prone to accept warnings about the music they listen to if they realize that the counsel is designed to maintain their God-given sensitivity to the whisperings of the Spirit, not to hamper their enjoyment of music.

Lucifer still employs the mist of the first temptation. It has served him well from the earliest ages of man through the present time. He changes its adaptation from age to age, but its essentials remain the same. Whenever we feel inclined to rebel or murmur over a given counsel because we feel our freedom is somehow being infringed upon, we would do well to remember the Garden of Eden with its many trees and ask ourselves which ones we are looking at.

TO ACT OR BE ACTED UPON

Lucifer deals in extremes. If he cannot push us to one end of the continuum, he will push us to the other. It is not surprising, therefore, that there are situations where he will deny the principles of freedom, choice, and accountability. This mist is usually used when someone is fighting a habit or lifestyle that is difficult to overcome but condemned by the Lord. Homosexuality is the most common example of this in today's society. We hear many voices that insist people are born that way and cannot choose to be otherwise.

I had a long discussion one afternoon with a student who was fighting this problem. He had read much literature that suggested he had no real power to resist these feelings and that sexual preference was not right or wrong but a matter of personality and genetics. Up to this point in his life he had not acted upon any of these feelings, but if he accepted these voices, he would stop resisting and assume a different behavior pattern. Together we turned to the teachings of Lehi, who supplied the mist-clearing truths that helped him continue his personal battle.

Lehi divided all things of creation into two categories: "There is a God, and he hath created all things, both the heavens and the earth, and all things that in them are, *both things to act and things to be acted upon.*" Lehi then added an important truth: "God gave unto man that he should *act* for himself." (2 Nephi 2:14, 16.) Things that are acted upon are those aspects of creation that have no agency or will. Much of nature falls into this category. In some ways man is also acted upon. Natural laws such as gravity exert their forces upon us, but in terms of moral choices we can act for ourselves. To emphasize this truth, Lehi later stated that the "children of men . . . have become *free* forever, knowing good from evil; *to act for themselves and not to be acted upon.* . . . Wherefore, men are *free* according to the flesh; and all things are given them which are expedient unto man. And they are *free* to *choose* liberty and eternal life, through the great Mediator of all men, or to *choose* captivity and death, according to the captivity and power of the devil." (2 Nephi 2:26–27.) Notice the key words that refute the ideas my young friend was hearing—*free, act, choose.*

We then turned to the writings of Jacob, who added a second

witness to the testimony of his father: "Therefore, cheer up your hearts, and remember that ye are *free to act for yourselves—* to *choose* the way of everlasting death or the way of eternal life." (2 Nephi 10:23.) Speaking from past ages, Lehi and Jacob told this student, "You are free! You can choose! You can act and not be acted upon!" He believed these two ancient prophets and as a result found strength to combat the influences that would have destroyed his eternal potential.

One critical circumstance when Lehi's and Jacob's testimonies needed to be believed involved a young woman who had been the victim of abuse as a child. This is a devastating influence to overcome and demands our deepest sympathies, but even here the assurance must be given that insecurities, fears, emotions, and personality patterns can be overcome. A normal life is possible. This young woman was struggling in her marriage as a result of her past abuse. Her husband tried to be understanding but did not know how to react to his wife's constant tensions relating to her trauma as a child. She felt powerless to change, wanting those around her to understand her pain and accept her. It took great love and patience, but in time, because she too believed Lehi and Jacob, trust and tenderness were restored, and a normal marriage relationship developed.

YOU CAN CHANGE

We live in a society in which, more and more, people refuse to take responsibility for their actions. Blame is transferred in any number of ways. "It's not my fault that I am the way I am," people say. Usually this becomes the excuse for giving in, for ending the battles, for refusing to take control of one's own life, for avoiding necessary changes. I came from a family where the parents were divorced. My sisters and I sometimes felt that our parents' decisions had created problems for us. Our personalities and characters were formed and set by our environment.

However, when any of us tried to excuse our behavior by suggesting that we had no power to change, our mother would say, "If you don't like you the way you are, you can change. You can be anything you want to be. You were God's child before you were mine."

Jacob believed that this truth produced great joy. "Cheer up your hearts," he told his people when he testified of their freedom to act. When making decisions about our agency, let us not move to either extreme as Lucifer would have us do. Joy will be the reward of staying in balance. Freedom must have some restrictions, yet they are placed for our protection and leave many wonderful fruits to taste. But there are no boundaries that limit our ability to act for ourselves in throwing off crippling habits or the pains of past trials. Lucifer would have us reverse the order and rebel against God's boundaries while accepting as final the destructive patterns or difficult challenges of our lives. We need not succumb to either mist. We may cheer up our hearts, secure in the clear vision of freedom the scriptures provide.

DECISIONS OF FREEDOM OR CHARITY

There is another way Lucifer uses the idea of freedom to disrupt the Church. From time to time differences of opinion among the members arise regarding various issues. Many of these are not particularly critical. They may have to do with various styles of clothing or grooming, different interpretations of the strictness of the Word of Wisdom, or the ratings of movies that one should see. This presents the opportunity for one side to judge the other while the other side claims that these issues are a matter of personal preference. Some examples are: Is it all right to drink Coca-Cola? Do shorts compromise the wearing of temple garments? Aren't PG-13 rated movies okay to see? Should a man's hair be cut short, or is it all right if it's long? Can a man wear a beard, or should all be clean-shaven? Is putting five dollars in an office tournament pool gambling? Other questions may concern the length of women's dresses, men wearing earrings, the choice of teenage music, wearing ties and white shirts on Sunday, and so on.

In the early Christian church, the Apostle Paul faced similar types of questions arising from the Jewish or Gentile backgrounds of his converts. Some converts would not eat certain types of meat. Some would eat only vegetables. Certain days were sacred holidays to some, but to others all days were the same. There was also a question of eating meat offered in sacrifice to the Greek and Roman gods. What was a Christian to do if invited to a nonbelieving friend's house where meat offered to an idol was served? Was it all right to buy such meat in the marketplace? For many Christians, who knew that the Greek and Roman gods did not exist, what did it matter if they ate the meat? They were free to do what they wanted in these areas, were they not? These questions may sound strange and trivial to us, but they caused problems for the early Saints.

Paul gave this counsel to those who were judging their fellow Saints for eating meat: "Why dost thou judge thy brother? or why dost thou set at nought thy brother? for we shall all stand before the judgment seat of Christ. . . . Let us not therefore judge one another any more." (Romans 14:10, 13.) These matters were between the individual and God. Using this standard, Paul says to us, "If your neighbor wants to wear a beard, or drink Coke, or see a certain movie, you are not to judge. That is between your neighbor and the Lord."

He then counseled those who claimed freedom in making these decisions, "If thy brother be grieved with thy meat, thou walkest not *charitably* if thou eatest. Therefore destroy not him with thy meat, for whom Christ died. . . . For the kingdom of God is not meat and drink; but righteousness, and peace, and joy in the Holy Ghost. . . . Let us therefore follow after the things which make for peace, and things wherewith one may edify another. . . . It is good neither to eat flesh, nor to drink wine, nor anything whereby thy brother stumbleth, or is offended, or is made weak. . . . Let every one of us *please his neighbor for his good to edification.*" (JST, Romans 14:15–15:2.) So, according to Paul, there are good reasons to abstain from things that are open to question.

WOUNDING ANOTHER'S CONSCIENCE

In his counsel to the Corinthian Saints, Paul added another reason not to exercise their freedom of choice in these matters. Some, he argued, may eat meat because of the examples of other Saints, or through peer pressure, but feel it is wrong. Thus, they would violate and weaken their consciences. "Take heed," Paul exhorted, "lest by any means this *liberty of yours* become a stumbling block to them that are weak." (1 Corinthians 8:9.) One violation may lead to another, impairing their power to resist in the future. "When ye sin so against the brethren, and wound their weak conscience, ye sin against Christ." Paul then concluded that for himself, "If meat make my brother to offend, I will eat no flesh while the world standeth, lest I make my brother to offend." (1 Corinthians 8:12–13.) He followed up this statement with a personal example. He could live off the donations of the Church if he chose to. He had a right to do this, as other apostles were doing. But he worked to support himself, lest others think he was preaching for selfish reasons, which would minimize his effectiveness.

The decision should be one of charity, love, peace, and unity rather than one of freedom, independence, rights, or our own feeling that there really isn't anything wrong with what we are doing. If we apply Paul's standard to the issues discussed above, decisions of charity could be easily made. "If my beard is troublesome to other members of the ward, then I'll shave it off," one might say. The teenage priest, knowing that his long hair was causing problems, would get a haircut. Paraphrasing Paul, another would say, "I will wear no shorts while the world stands, lest I make my brother to offend." Knowing that some members of a youth group felt that the language or suggestiveness in a popular movie was wrong, the others would not rent it, so their friends would not, through peer pressure or curiosity, compromise their consciences. "I can drink 7-Up instead of Pepsi," one might say. "Unity among the other members is of greater value to me than a soft drink." A young woman, understanding that some of her clothing was seen by some to border on the immodest, would willingly change styles: "A few inches on a skirt is not as important to me as the feelings of the other members of my ward." Regrettably, however, we sometimes think, "There's nothing wrong with what I'm doing, so others will just have to live with it. It's really none of their business anyway."

It is difficult to think in the manner Paul is suggesting. With our sense of freedom, we have great resistance to living our lives with this much concern for the feelings and sensitivities of others. The American character in particular responds negatively to this challenge to its liberty. Of course, the need to be conscious of others' feelings cannot be considered when the question in debate involves true decisions of right and wrong. One cannot do wrong for the sake of peace, unity, and sensitivity to friends. That thought in itself is a temptation of Lucifer discussed in another chapter.

As with all principles, we can push this one too far, but Paul has given us mist-clearing wisdom that would be of great benefit to the Church if followed. We must also remember that Paul strongly instructed the Saints not to judge one another in these matters. According to his epistle, it is equally wrong for the member who does not wear shorts, or watch PG-13 movies, or drink Coke to condemn those who do. Charity must be the guiding principle for both sides. If it is, we will learn, as Paul testifies, that "the kingdom of God is not meat and drink; but

righteousness, and peace, and joy in the Holy Ghost." (Romans
14:17.) The blessings for decisions of charity above decisions of
freedom will be an increase in our own individual sensitivity to
the Holy Ghost as well as greater spiritual power in the broader
Church.

CHAPTER FOUR

DON'T GO TO CAIAPHAS' PALACE

Peter had a deep and abiding love for the Savior, as he demonstrated time and time again. His testimony was unquestioned, although he had a great deal to learn about the Savior's true mission. This he would learn, and he would become the powerful leader we read of in the Acts of the Apostles. It is important to remember how devoted he was and how strong a testimony he bore on numerous occasions in order to understand the full power of his experiences on the night of Christ's arrest.

"YET WILL I NEVER"

During the Last Supper, Jesus addressed Peter with the following warning: "Simon, Simon, Satan hath desired you, that he may sift the children of the kingdom as wheat. But I have prayed for thee, that thy faith fail not: and when thou art converted, strengthen thy brethren." (JST, Luke 22:31–32.) I am sure Peter felt he was already "converted" and strong enough to face the coming tests. He replied, "Lord, I am ready to go with thee, both into prison, and to death." (Luke 22:33.) According to Matthew and Mark's version of the Last Supper,

Jesus also announced to the disciples, "All ye shall be offended because of me this night." (Matthew 26:31; Mark 14:27.) Unable to comprehend his own vulnerability, Peter replied, "Though *all men* shall be offended because of thee, *yet will I never* be offended." (Matthew 26:33.)

In Peter's own assessment of his courage, devotion, and strength, it was simply not conceivable that he could be offended or shy away from death or imprisonment if his faith in his master was put to the test. Others might, in their weakness, deny or flee, but "never" would this happen to Peter. This overconfidence became his mist. In response to Peter's assertion, Jesus warned, "Verily I say unto thee, That this night, before the cock crow, thou shalt deny me thrice." (Matthew 26:34.)

None of us may be as strong as we believe we are when placed in certain tempting or pressured situations, yet we often say words similar to those of Peter. I recall a conversation I had with a teenage couple who in high school were going steady. They were both active and committed young Latter-day Saints. They spent considerable time with each other, both in person and on the phone. The weekends were occupied in dating and spending time at each other's houses. They simply couldn't understand why their parents were so afraid that they would have moral problems. "We know other teenagers have these problems," they said, "but we are strong enough to resist the temptations." I could hear Peter's voice echoed in their words.

Many parents, faced with similar challenges, hear their children ask, "Don't you trust me?" I have found that the best answer to that question is, "No. I don't trust myself in certain situations. Greater than both of us have fallen."

If Peter had conceived that it was possible for him, in spite of his own perceived strength, to actually deny his Master, I wonder where he would have gone that night, when Christ was arrested in the Garden of Gethsemane. Perhaps he would have gone home, locked himself in his closet, and told his wife not to let anyone near him until she heard the cock crow. He would have done all in his power to avoid a situation that would give him the opportunity to fulfill the Savior's warning. However, blinded by the mist of his own strength, he went to the worst possible place that night—Caiaphas' palace.

CAIAPHAS' PALACE

Since John was also in the palace, he gives us the fullest version of Peter's three denials. To understand the pressures on Peter, we must remember that earlier, when the officers came to arrest Jesus, Peter had drawn a sword, attacked one of the arresting party (the servant of the high priest), and cut off his ear. This could hardly be seen as a legal or justifiable act, and although Jesus healed the stricken servant, in the volatile world of the New Testament, Peter could stand accused of wrongdoing. In spite of this action, when they led Jesus away, Peter followed.

At Caiaphas' palace a young woman, acting under the prompting of John, who "was known unto the high priest," let Peter in. "Art not thou also one of this man's disciples?" she asked. "I am not," Peter replied. (John 18:16–17.) It does not appear that there was tremendous pressure on Peter in this first instance, especially in light of the fact that John appears to have been standing nearby, but Peter denied nonetheless. Perhaps he was afraid she would not let him into the palace courtyard if he admitted he was a disciple.

Peter moved to warm himself by a fire, where we are specifically told that the same "servants and officers" who had earlier arrested Jesus were standing. (John 18:18.) The circumstances for his second denial were different. The pressure would be greater with the officers than with the young woman. When confronted with their accusations, he denied a second time.

The third denial also involved a change of circumstances

that would understandably put more pressure on Peter. "One of the servants of the high priest, *being his kinsman whose ear Peter cut off,* saith, Did not I see thee in the garden with him? Peter then denied again: and immediately the cock crew." (John 18:26–27.) At this moment Luke tells us that Jesus looked upon Peter, which caused Peter to leave the palace, and he "wept bitterly." (Luke 22:62.)

I have often wondered what Peter thought after each denial. Did he feel sorrow or guilt? Did he rationalize or excuse himself based on the situation? Did he vow to himself, as we often do after our own weaknesses are revealed, that the next time he would be stronger? But the next time, he was confronted with increasing pressure in the form of officers and finally a kinsman. We cannot know the answers to these questions, but we can learn from Peter that it is best to stay away from the Caiaphas' palaces of our own lives, lest a unique and unpredictable set of circumstances confront us and we discover, as did Peter, that we are not really stronger than "all men."

"IT WILL NEVER HAPPEN TO ME"

I do not judge or condemn Peter, but I am grateful for the honesty of all four Gospel writers who gave us details of Peter's night of self-discovery. When I was a young man, my best friend went to "Caiaphas' palace" one time too many. He was popular, dated often, and pushed the limits of propriety with his dates, many of whom were not Latter-day Saints and did not share gospel standards. I remember one evening when we had a serious conversation about our futures and his present actions. He deeply desired to fulfill a mission. He wanted a temple marriage. I pointed out to him that he often went dangerously close to the edge in his moral behavior. I will never forget his reply: "It will never happen to me. I know just how far to go and when to quit."

Our senior year, blinded by the mists of his own confidence, he found himself in a situation he could not handle; his girlfriend became pregnant, and he left school to marry her and support his child. I did not see him for months, in spite of my efforts to talk with him. I went to college for a year and then returned home to serve a mission. While sitting on the stand at my farewell, I saw him enter the back of the chapel and sit down. He waited there for me until everyone had left and we were alone. With his eyes downcast, he shook my hand and gave me a twenty-dollar bill. "Serve a mission for both of us," he said. Then he turned and walked out of the chapel.

"BOASTING IN THY STRENGTH AND WISDOM"

Alma the Younger must have been thinking of this type of mist when counseling his youngest son, Corianton, who had been to the "land of Siron after the harlot Isabel." For Alma's son, "the land of Siron" was a Caiaphas' palace. Alma pinpointed his son's problem when he said, "Now this is what I have against thee; thou didst *go on unto boasting in thy strength and thy wisdom.*" (Alma 39:2–3.)

In the play *A Man for All Seasons,* Sir Thomas More, knowing the ambitious inclinations of Richard Rich, gave him counsel that is good for all of us to heed. He advised, "A man should go where he won't be tempted." (Robert Bolt, *A Man for All Seasons* [New York: Scholastic Book Services, 1960], p. 5.) Richard refused More's wisdom and, as More feared, lost his soul as well as bringing about Sir Thomas More's own death.

There are many different Caiaphas' palaces that we may encounter. Lest we be tempted as Richard Rich, we must do what we can to avoid them. I have seen people entangled deeply in the pursuit of wealth. In their earlier years they were generous and committed to their families and the Church. They would never have conceived in those years that money could gain such a grasp upon them. We may simply not be as strong as we believe.

If someone had suggested to the young David that later in life he would commit adultery with a faithful follower's wife and then have his follower killed, I am sure he would not have believed it. If someone had suggested to Solomon on the day he dedicated the temple to Jehovah that one day he would allow people to build altars for the sacrifice of infants, he would surely have thought it impossible. If these powerful and righteous leaders may fall, we would be wise to keep in mind our own fallibility and do all we can to avoid Caiaphas' palace. There is safety in going only where we won't be tempted.

Peter, James, and John accompanied Jesus to the summit of the Mount of Transfiguration and experienced wonderful things. There they saw Jesus in His glory, flanked by Elijah and Moses. There they heard the voice of God and felt the power of His presence. At the climax of this spiritual outpouring, Peter said, "Lord, it is good for us to be here." (Matthew 17:4.) Let us be guided by that powerful statement and go only to those places where we too may say, "It is good for us to be here." From such heights we are in some measure immune from the mists that hang thickly in the valleys below.

CHAPTER FIVE

THE SAFEST PLACE IN THE WORLD

When I was a boy working on my uncle's ranch, he used to say to me, "The safest place in the world is the back of a horse!" I had ample opportunities to prove the validity of his claim. One summer day we rode onto the desert looking for cattle we had missed in the previous year's branding. We found a number of them, including a bull that had never seen riders on horseback before. He was wild and uncontrollable and charged our horses. We finally put him in a larger herd, which calmed him down enough for us to drive him to the ranch. During the trip I lost all fear of him.

When we arrived, my uncle instructed me to ride ahead of the herd, open the gate, get behind the cattle again, and drive them into the corral. He would occupy himself with other chores. As a parting instruction he reminded me of how wild the bull was, followed by his customary advice: "Remember, the safest place in the world is the back of a horse."

I did as he instructed, but the bull would not cooperate. Time and time again he backed away from the gate, refusing to enter the corral. He backed himself into a corner where two fence lines met and defied me to make him move. In full frustration, I made my first big mistake—I got off my horse. Climbing over one of the fences so it was between me and the bull, I poked him with a stick and pounded on him in order to make him move. Resolutely he stood his ground. I climbed back over the fence, took a position ten yards in front of him, picked up a rock the size of a hardball, and threw it at him with all my might. Now the only time in my life I have actually hit exactly what I was aiming at was right then. The rock struck him in the center of his nose, where all the nerve endings in a bull's body meet.

Now he moved! For a split second I stood frozen in fear, then turned and ran for the closest fence. I remember, as I was running, seeing my horse out of the corner of my eye. Of course, it was too late to get back on him, but I would have given anything to be in the safety of the saddle again. With the extra energy of fear I was able to leap the fence and roll to safety on the other side just as the bull crashed into it.

The Lord has prepared for His children a powerful horse to ride. It consists of councils and commandments, honor codes, standards, and the insights of prophets and apostles. As long as we stay on that horse, we are safe. I have found that the adversary, like the bull, often waits patiently for the right opportunity to come. He charges when we are most vulnerable, and he often comes with all his power, hoping to run us over in one attack. Safety lies in following my uncle's words: "The safest place in the world is the back of a horse."

LEHONTI'S MOUNTAIN

This principle is taught throughout the scriptures. In the 47th chapter of Alma we are introduced to the treacherous ways of Amalickiah. Since evil people, such as Amalickiah, are influenced by the adversary, we can learn a great deal about Satan's tactics through examining the behavior of his followers, just as we learn much about the Savior by studying those who truly follow Him. Amalickiah is described as "being a very subtle man to do evil." (Alma 47:4.)

Fleeing to the Lamanites after being repulsed by the actions of Captain Moroni, he stirred them up to anger and was placed at the head of the Lamanite armies. There was only one problem for him to overcome: A large portion of the Lamanites didn't want to go to war. Their leader was a man named Lehonti. He gathered his followers "upon the top of the mount which was called Antipas." (Alma 47:7.) Here they would make their stand, "being *fixed* in their minds with a *determined resolution* that they would not be *subjected* to go against the Nephites." (Alma 47:6.)

Notice the three powerful words that suggest to us how strongly they were committed to their stand. There may be times in our own lives when we feel this same commitment against the temptations of the adversary or the pressures of the world. We are fixed, determined, and resolute that we will not be subjected by the world or Lucifer. We camp out on the top of our spiritual Mount Antipas, confident in our position of safety. Then comes the invitation to come down.

WHO IS IN CONTROL?

Three times Amalickiah sent word to Lehonti to "come down" and converse with him. With his fixed resolution not to be deceived, Lehonti "durst not go down." (Alma 47:11.) Now the subtle evil of Amalickiah becomes apparent. He must convince Lehonti that if he comes down, he will still be in control of the situation. "When Amalickiah found that he could not get Lehonti to come down off from the mount, he went up into the mount, nearly to Lehonti's camp; and he sent again the fourth time his message unto Lehonti, desiring that he would come down, and that he would bring his guards with him." (Alma 47:12.)

"You're in control! I only want to talk! You have your guards!

You only have to come down a little bit!" Amalickiah assures his victim. Lehonti, feeling secure although undoubtedly mistrustful, made his first mistake: He descended from the heights of the mountain. In his own mind, however, he was still safe, because he was in control.

An agreement was reached between the two leaders. If Lehonti came down in the night and surrounded Amalickiah's forces, they would be delivered into Lehonti's power. In exchange, Amalickiah would be made second in command. Notice again how Amalickiah assured Lehonti that he was in control of the situation. The bargain was struck, and Lehonti descended to the foot of the mount.

What is Lucifer's tactic with those who won't "come down" from the spiritual heights of Antipas? He must give them the impression that if they come down, they will still be in control of the situation. The fatal fallacy is to think you are ever in control when you descend to the foot of the mountain. Lehonti lost control when he descended the first few feet, but only Amalickiah was aware of this. It would be only a matter of time before the full tragedy of Lehonti's mistake was played out.

POISON BY DEGREES

"And it came to pass that Amalickiah caused that one of his servants should administer *poison by degrees* to Lehonti, that he died." (Alma 47:18.) Once we are off the mount, it is a simple matter for the adversary to use one of his most effective methods. He poisons by degrees, so slowly that his victims are unaware of their own spiritual decline. Lehonti died still believing he was in control. Cain was deceived in a similar manner. Notice what Satan did just prior to Cain's forming of the first secret combination: "Satan sware unto Cain *that he would do according to his commands.*" (Moses 5:30.) Cain could dominate the relationship; Lucifer would be very obedient.

A young man who had developed a destructive habit with

pornography, one of Satan's most deadly poisons, could bear witness of Lehonti's problem in his own life. He had been raised by parents whose standards for movies were those found in *For the Strength of Youth,* not the ratings of Hollywood. Entertainment in his family was built on the Mount Antipas of "Don't attend or participate in any form of entertainment, including concerts, movies, and videocassettes, that is *vulgar, immoral, inappropriate, suggestive, or pornographic in any way.*" (*For the Strength of Youth* [Salt Lake City: The Church of Jesus Christ of Latter-day Saints, 1990], pp. 11–12.) What value do PG, PG-13, or R ratings have in the face of the Lord's rating system?

However, a popular movie came out that everyone was seeing. His friends urged him to accompany them. "It was not rated R," he reasoned, "and if there are any scenes that are compromising, I can always get up and leave." He felt completely in control. From that first descent from the standards he was raised on, he was slowly poisoned by degrees until he found himself with a vicious habit made ever more accessible with the development of the Internet.

PILATE'S FOLLY

In light of Lehonti's fatal decisions, Pontius Pilate's role in the death of the Savior is instructive. He made the common mistake of believing he could compromise with evil. "I need to come down the mountain only a few feet." A little equivocation will satisfy the unrighteous demands of others or the insistent desires of our own wills. Pilate "was determined to let [Jesus] go." (Acts 3:13.) "For he knew that for envy they had delivered him." (Matthew 27:18.) He had even been encouraged in this decision by his wife, who told him of a dream. "Have thou nothing to do with that just man," she counseled. (Matthew 27:19.) He had every reason and support to do what was right. After examining Jesus, Pilate passed judgment: "I find

no fault in this man." (Luke 23:4.) Now was the critical
moment to stand firm.

Pilate was powerful, but the opponents of the Savior were
insistent. Perhaps if he gave them a little of what they wanted,
they would be satisfied. His first step down the road of compromise was to pass the responsibility of judgment to Herod. When
that did not work, he took his next step. He would condemn
Jesus, as they wanted, but then pardon Him according to the
custom of the feast. Would not this satisfy everyone? The pressure on him to capitulate only intensified as the cry went up to
release Barabbas instead of Jesus.

He tried another approach. He would condemn Jesus but
give Him a lesser sentence than death. He scourged Him and
then brought Him out to the people with the crown of thorns
and the purple robe. Surely the kinder sympathies of the rulers
would now be satisfied, and Jesus could be released. "Behold
the man!" Pilate cried. "Crucify him, crucify him," the crowd
replied. Pilate said, "Take ye him, and crucify him: for I find no
fault in him." (John 19:5–6.)

Returning to Jesus, Pilate examined Him again, looking for
a way to save a man he knew was innocent. Once again he
brought Him before the people. He would appeal to their
national pride. "Behold your King! . . . Shall I crucify your
King? We have no king but Caesar," they answered. (John
19:14–15.) In the end Pilate relented, washing his hands in a
gesture of relinquishing responsibility.

When courage is demanded, compromise and evasion is not
enough. Equivocation only whets appetite. Evil is never satisfied, but the adversary will try to deceive us into thinking that
giving in a little will ease the pressure. It never does. This is one
of his more deceptive means of poisoning by degrees. The
young woman who thinks her boyfriend will stop pushing the
limits of intimacy if she lowers her standards just a bit is
committing Pilate's mistake. The man who believes he will be

satisfied with one more possession, the nicer car, the newer house, the RV, the big-screen TV, the Jet Ski, or the last big stock trade may one day discover that Pilate's folly has caught up with him as he moves farther and farther down the road of materialism, or deeper and deeper into the captivity of debt. Power, position, lust, gluttony, and many other temptations work this way. Even in terms of losing faith, the poison can come slowly by degrees. Do not the scriptures speak of "dwindling" in unbelief?

HELAMAN'S FORMULA
FOR REMAINING FIXED

Since both Lehonti and Pilate are described as being "fixed and determined" in their decisions and yet eventually gave in, what can we do to remain true to our predetermined convictions? Helaman, while fighting with the stripling warriors, gives us a clue.

Helaman was leading an army that was "not strong, according to . . . numbers" (Alma 58:15) and had to "contend with an enemy which was innumerable" (Alma 58:8). Viewing the odds, he knew he needed additional strength, but the Nephite government "did not send more strength." (Alma 58:9.) They would have to make their determined stand alone.

"Therefore, *we did pour out our souls in prayer to God, that he would strengthen us and deliver us.*" (Alma 58:10.) It is not always enough to climb to the top of Lehonti's mountain; deep prayer is also required. Notice what four things came as a result of their prayers: "The Lord our God did visit us with *assurances* that he would deliver us; yea, insomuch that he did speak *peace* to our souls, and did grant unto us *great faith*, and did cause us that we should *hope* for our deliverance in him." (Alma 58:11.) When we face innumerable forces that attempt to get us to come down from our places of security in spite of our resoluteness, if we pray deeply for strength, the Lord will bless us, too, with assurances, peace, great faith, and hope. These are especially needed in the latter days, for Nephi "beheld the church of the Lamb of God, and its numbers were few," just like Helaman's army. (1 Nephi 14:12.)

Filled with the comfort of these four things, Helaman's men "did take *courage*." With this new infusion of courage, they were now "*fixed with a determination* to conquer [their] enemies, and to *maintain* [their] . . . cause of [their] liberty. And thus [they] did go forth with *all [their] might*." (Alma 58:12–13.)

Helaman has provided us with an effective formula. Prayer leads to assurance, peace, great faith, and hope, which create the courage necessary for us to remain fixed and determined in maintaining our spiritual liberty. Now we can battle the adversary "with all our might."

THE PLAIN OF ONO

Amalickiah's four invitations to Lehonti to "come down" from the mount remind us of another person in the scriptures who received a similar invitation. But the outcome of his story is much different. From Nehemiah we learn of a powerful defense that, when added to our prayers, will repel the subtle suggestions and clear the mists that lead so often to poisoning by degrees.

Nehemiah was a Jewish official in the service of the Persian court when he heard that the walls of Jerusalem, which had been destroyed in an earlier generation by the Babylonians, were still in ruins. Moved by the Spirit and his concern for his people, he petitioned the king to allow him to return to rebuild the walls. Once the effort was begun, tremendous opposition surfaced, which Nehemiah had to overcome. His chief adversaries were Sanballat, Tobiah, and Geshem. Like Amalickiah in the Book of Mormon, these three would try to get Nehemiah to "come down."

"Sanballat and Geshem sent unto me, saying, Come, let us

meet together in some one of the villages in the plain of Ono. But they thought to do me mischief." (Nehemiah 6:2.) There is wonderful irony in the name of the plain these men wanted Nehemiah to descend to in order to "do him mischief." When we read of this plain, we might emphasize its pronunciation as the plain of *Oh, no!* On the plain of *Oh, no!* we are sure to meet with mischief. It is helpful every now and then to examine our lives and try to determine where the plain of Ono is located for us.

However, in contrast with Lehonti, Nehemiah could not be deceived: "I sent messengers unto them, saying, I am doing a *great work,* so that I cannot come down: why should the work cease, whilst I *leave it,* and come down to you? Yet they sent unto me four times after this sort; and I answered them after the same manner." (Nehemiah 6:3–4.)

A great key to avoiding the plain of Ono is to be engaged in a great work. Perhaps this is one of the reasons the Lord constantly calls His latter-day work of restoration "a marvelous work." We must fill our lives so full of good things that there is no room for compromises. Hence the Lord encourages us in the 13th article of faith to "seek after"—not just wait for them to come to us—those things that are "virtuous, lovely, or of good report or praiseworthy." This truth is so important that it was taught in the very first chapters of revealed scripture. The Lord told Cain, "If thou *doest well,* thou shalt be accepted. And if *thou doest not well, sin lieth at the door,* and Satan desireth to have thee." (Moses 5:23.)

It is not enough to climb to the top of Mount Antipas and there resolutely refuse to come down. We must be doing something while we're up there. Like Nehemiah, we must participate in a great work. The more engaging and wonderful the work, the less likely we will be to leave it.

Jesus told a parable about the critical need to fill our lives with positive, righteous things in order to keep evil out: "When the unclean spirit is gone out of a man, he walketh through dry places, seeking rest, and findeth none. Then he saith, I will return into my house from whence I came out; and when he is come, he findeth it *empty*, swept and garnished. Then goeth he, and taketh with himself seven other spirits more wicked than himself, and they enter in and dwell there." (Matthew 12:43–45.)

The key word in the parable is *empty*. The house was swept and garnished with the understanding that the Spirit of the Lord would move in. The empty house must be filled with so many good things that there is no room for the evil to return. The best defense is a good offense in this matter.

DOING A GREAT WORK

One afternoon while reflecting on Nehemiah's wisdom, I discovered a unique application to his counsel. I asked myself what great wall-building work I was engaged in from which the adversary might wish to divert me. Several answers ran through my mind until finally I settled upon the thoughts of eternal relationships—those that can be forged only in the temples of the Most High.

As a husband, what greater work could I accomplish than building an eternal marriage in a world where so much pressure tears at the unity of husbands and wives? "Treat your spouse in such a way that the thought of spending eternity without him or her is painful to contemplate," the Lord might say. Surely there is no greater work than the forging of two independent souls into one eternal companionship.

As a father, what greater work could I accomplish than raising children of integrity, dignity, and righteousness in a world slipping ever deeper into degradation? As a son and grandson, what greater work could I accomplish than tying generations together through honor, sacrifice, obedience, and respect?

Another great work involves reaching through the veil of

should obey his voice to let Israel go? I know not the Lord, neither will I let Israel go." (Exodus 5:2.)

A second time the request was made for time to worship: "Let us go, we pray thee, three days' journey into the desert, and sacrifice unto the Lord our God." (Exodus 5:3.)

Pharaoh's solution to this request for freedom to worship and sacrifice to God was an effective one: "Wherefore do ye, Moses and Aaron, let [stop] the people from their works? *get you unto your burdens.* . . . The people of the land now are many, and ye make them *rest* from their burdens. . . . Let there *more work* be laid upon the men, that they may labour therein; and let them not regard vain words." (Exodus 5:4–5, 9.) The command was then issued for the people to gather their own straw, the idea being that if they had time to think about worshiping their God or desired a day of rest, they were not busy enough.

"And the taskmasters hasted them, saying, Fulfil your works, your daily tasks. . . . Ye are idle, ye are idle: therefore ye say, Let us go and do sacrifice to the Lord. Go therefore now, and work." (Exodus 5:13, 17–18.)

OUR DAILY BREAD AND MORE

The modern work ethic is a good thing, but, as in all things, it can be pushed too far. The Savior prayed that we should be given our "daily bread," but often we want it buttered and covered with jam, which requires more and more work. Our "daily tasks," like those of the Israelites, seem to stretch and grow and fill more and more of our time, leaving less time for much-needed worship, rest, and sacrifice to God. We find ourselves, either through the demands of the world or our own desires for more, making bricks without straw.

During the time of Malachi, the Israelite priesthood was not offering to God the honor, respect, or sacrifices worthy of his service. In response the Lord asked them a question I have often pondered myself. "Offer it now unto thy governor; will he be pleased with thee, or accept thy person?" (Malachi 1:8.) In other words, if I did my temporal work with the same diligence that I fulfill my religious obligations, would my employer give me a raise or fire me?

I was interested in a study that was discussed during a recent news broadcast. Several decades ago, business, governmental, and scientific leaders were forecasting that, with the increase of technology, the time demands on American workers would decrease, leaving them with more time to pursue personal and family interests. However, just the opposite is happening. Instead of spending less time earning "our daily bread," the length of the work week and the hours of labor expected is increasing, pushing into evening hours and weekends to a greater and greater extent.

President Gordon B. Hinckley has on a number of occasions counseled the Saints on the need to take three days' journey into the desert and sacrifice to the Lord. "We need to build ourselves spiritually," he has said. "We live in a world of rush and go, of running here and there and in every direction. We are very busy people. We have so much to do. We need to get off by ourselves once in a while and think of spiritual things and build ourselves spiritually. . . . Get by yourself and think of things of the Lord, of things of the Spirit. . . . Just meditate and reflect for an hour about yourself and your relationship to your Heavenly Father and your Redeemer. It will do something for you." (*Teachings of Gordon B. Hinckley* [Salt Lake City: Deseret Book Co., 1977], pp. 608–9.)

President David O. McKay believed that meditation is a form of prayer and a critical factor in our attempts to overcome Satan's influences in our lives. In one of his conference addresses he spoke on this subject: "Meditation is one of the most secret, most sacred doors through which we pass into the presence of the Lord. Jesus set the example for us. As soon as he was baptized and received the Father's approval . . . Jesus repaired to what is now known as the mount of temptation. I like to think of it as the mount of meditation where, during the forty days of fasting, he communed with himself and his Father, and contemplated upon the responsibility of his great mission. One result of this spiritual communion was *such strength as enabled him to say to the tempter: get thee hence Satan.*" (In Conference Report, April 1946, p. 113.) With this result from quiet time for deep mediation, it is little wonder Lucifer would keep us so busy, so surrounded with noise and rush that this great barrier to his influences may be checked.

SHOUTING DOWN THE MELODIES OF HEAVEN

C. S. Lewis described the brick-making tactic of the world in *The Screwtape Letters.* His chief protagonist in this book is a devil giving instructions on how to destroy faith: "We will make the whole universe a noise in the end. We have already made great strides in this direction as regards the Earth. The melodies and silences of Heaven will be shouted down in the end." (*The Screwtape Letters* [New York: The Macmillan Co., 1973], p. 103.)

The Savior related a parable that gives further insight into the brick-making tendencies of life: "A certain man made a great supper, and bade many: and sent his servant at supper time to say to them that were bidden, Come; for all things are now ready. And they all with one consent began to make excuse. The first said unto him, I have bought a piece of ground, and I must needs go and see it: I pray thee have me excused. And another said, I have bought five yoke of oxen, and I go to prove them: I pray thee have me excused. And another said, I have married a wife, and therefore I cannot come." (Luke 14:16–20.)

Our Father in Heaven has spread before us a rich feast of the most nourishing elements. He invites us all to partake. We find this feast in the temple, in the scriptures, in the counsels of apostles and prophets, during the sacrament, in the wonders and beauties of nature, in eternal family relationships, and in quiet, reflective moments of prayer. But Pharaoh's demands must be met. There are bricks to make, and oxen to prove, and ground that needs to be examined; time passes, and we miss so much that would contribute to the happiness and spiritual health of ourselves and our families.

ABUNDANCE OF IDLENESS

As we see so often when dealing with the mists of the adversary, if one mist cannot confuse and blind, its exact opposite may do the trick. Pharaoh accused the Israelites three times of being "idle"—hence his solution of more work. Yet idleness is an effective tool in its own right. It seems that we have either no free time to serve, reflect, and worship, or we have so much idle time that we get ourselves into mischief. Sodom, that great ancient playground of evil, was fueled by idleness: "Behold, this was the iniquity of thy sister Sodom, pride, fulness of bread, *and abundance of idleness was in her.*" (Ezekiel 16:49.)

"MY OWN TIME"

Another mist may surface in a life made heavy with brick-making. There may be times in our lives when we have worked so hard and been so busy that we consider any time left as our own. We may then feel annoyed or irritated when the Lord presses His own invitations and demands upon us. This can come on Monday night when we feel the responsibility to hold family home evening, at night before retiring when scripture reading and prayer seem to delay that well-deserved bed, or on Sunday with Church callings and meetings.

Of course, we must be careful to keep our Church callings and meetings in balance. Otherwise, we may find ourselves making Church bricks instead of attending to more critical family needs. Church bricks may be more beautiful than the temporal bricks of life, but they are bricks just the same if they keep us from more important responsibilities. We must also remember, however, that our time is not really our own but a gift from God, and we are stewards over this commodity as well as over our talents and resources. We must be careful not to think of the Lord's requests upon our time as impositions that get in the way of entertainment or worldly pleasures.

Isaiah had this in mind when he wrote, "If thou turn away thy foot from the sabbath, from doing thy pleasure on my holy day; and call the sabbath a delight, the holy of the Lord, honourable; and shalt honour him, not doing thine own ways, nor finding thine own pleasure, nor speaking thine own words: Then shalt thou delight thyself in the Lord." (Isaiah 58:13–14.)

As in most areas of our lives, as we try to continually find balance, we will need to listen to the wisdom of the Holy Spirit to make the right type of bricks in the right number at the right time. If we do this, all the buildings of our lives will reflect the beauty of the Lord.

CHAPTER SEVEN

SUFFERING FROM NOAH BLINDNESS

In an English class in high school, we studied the Greek play *Oedipus*. It is the tragic story of King Oedipus, who slowly discovers the truth about his past, which eventually leads him to blind himself. The scene where Oedipus destroys his ability to see disturbed me for some time. Eyesight is such a precious gift that to deliberately destroy it was deeply troubling. Ever since then I have not been able to enjoy or even reread Sophocles' play.

Seeing and blindness are used as symbols throughout the scriptures. Jesus in particular used the metaphor of sight frequently in His teachings, often emphasizing self-inflicted spiritual blindness. One of the most tragic types of self-deluding blindness I call "Noah blindness," after the story of King Noah in the Book of Mormon. It is a common problem and an effective mist of the adversary.

THE EYES OF THE PEOPLE

The whole story of King Noah is introduced with the idea of vision. The qualities of a seer are described in great detail in Mosiah, chapter 8. Then, in contrast, the people are described:

"O how marvelous are the works of the Lord, and how long doth he suffer with his people; yea, and how *blind and impenetrable* are the understandings of the children of men." (Mosiah 8:20.) The Lord is anxious that we understand the blindness of King Noah's people, and He sets the stage with this verse.

At his death, Zeniff turned the affairs of the Nephite kingdom in the land of Nephi over to his son Noah. Zeniff had been a righteous king, but Noah "changed the affairs of the kingdom." (Mosiah 11:4.) These changes were all for the worse. He threw out the old priests and picked new ones. He lived an immoral life with his concubines and became a "wine-bibber." He built spacious buildings and furnished them with luxurious furnishings for himself and his wicked priests. He fought with the Lamanites and returned "rejoicing in their spoil." (Mosiah 11:18.) All these excesses he supported by taxing the people one-fifth of all they had.

Often when we study the scriptures, it is important to focus on the common, unnamed people, the masses who form the backdrop for the major characters. Noah's people are an excellent example. Normally we would expect that a people supporting such evil and laziness would rebel or condemn their leaders, but Noah's people didn't seem to complain. Even though they did "labor exceedingly to support iniquity" (Mosiah 11:6), they weren't in any hurry to change the affairs of the kingdom back to the righteous ways of Zeniff.

Noah allowed the people to give in to the inclinations of the natural man, and his wicked priests justified it. In the eyes of the people, Noah could do no wrong. He was the best friend and leader the people ever had. When Abinadi entered the scene, calling both the leaders and the people to repentance, it was the people who challenged Abinadi: "They were wroth with him and sought to take away his life." (Mosiah 11:26.) At this point in the story, we are reminded once more of the theme of blindness; the last verse of chapter 11 says: "Now the eyes of the people were blinded; therefore they hardened their hearts against the words of Abinadi." (Mosiah 11:29.)

The people simply could not tell the difference between one who was their true friend—Abinadi—and those who were in reality their spiritual enemies, Noah and the priests. In life we often get confused about those people and influences that are our true friends or enemies. If we hope to avoid some fairly painful moments, we simply must learn to distinguish between the Noahs and the Abinadis of our lives.

DEFENDING THE ENEMY

Noah blindness is evidenced in our own lives when we can't see the danger or evil in our choice of friends, influences, ideas, or environments. Convinced that these people or ideas are good and proper, we see anyone who suggests otherwise as the enemy, and we defend the bad influences with much energy.

When Abinadi returned later to try again to convince the people of the dangers of Noah and his priests, the people arrested him and hauled him before the king, saying, "O king, what great evil hast thou done, or what great sins have thy people committed, that we should be condemned of God or judged of this man? And now, O king, behold, we are guiltless, and thou, O king, hast not sinned." (Mosiah 12:13–14.)

A common defense when others point out to us that we are suffering the symptoms of Noah blindness is to accuse them of judging. Perhaps some examples will be useful by way of illustration.

All parents pray that their children will associate with good friends. Friends can have a powerful influence for either good or bad. I know of a fine young man who formed a friendship with a group of boys whose standards were considerably lower than his. At first he resisted the temptation to participate in their activities or to dress and groom as they did. In time, however, his own behavior changed as well as his appearance. When his parents, youth leaders, and bishop pointed out to him the changes and the dangers, his reply was, "You don't really know them. You are judging them just because they have long hair." He was Noah-blind.

In another ward, my wife served as the Young Women president. When one of the Laurels graduated from high school, she began to date a young man who had Word of Wisdom problems and was completely inactive. Her first desire was to "save" him and bring him back into full Church activity. This was a noble goal; unfortunately, far too often those with the higher standards are pulled down, as was the case with this young woman. Once again concerned parents and leaders tried to help her see the changes in herself. In her strong defense of her new boyfriend, this girl saw her parents, the bishop, and my wife (formerly her close friend) as the enemy, just as Abinadi was the enemy in the eyes of Noah's people. She, too, was Noah-blind.

I knew a young man in college for whom a sophisticated and intelligent professor became a Noah. This professor constantly challenged the faith of this young Latter-day Saint. In time he lost his testimony, left all his old acquaintances, and changed his lifestyle to one involving destructive patterns. He defended himself and the professor as being "open-minded" as opposed to the "narrow-minded" attitudes of the LDS people.

Often rock music and the culture that accompanies it blind youth to its dangerous and damaging power. Yet many youth will defend such music as harmless. "You don't really understand," they often say to those who understand all too well the effects of Noah blindness.

NOAH MOMENTS—
SEEING IN THE WILDERNESS

Noah blindness usually does not last forever. Clear vision often returns, but the sight is many times uncomfortable. When we come out of a dark room into the bright sunlight, the result is painful at first. As a bishop, some of my most painful times were those shared with members who had been Noah-blind and then had their sight restored. I called these interviews "Noah moments."

When Abinadi spoke to the people the second time, he uttered an ironic prophesy: "The life of king Noah shall be valued even as a garment in a hot furnace." (Mosiah 12:3.) To understand the ironic power of this prophecy as it relates to Noah blindness, let us try to project ourselves into this story.

After the burning of Abinadi, the affairs of the kingdom began to go against Noah and his priests. One day a man named Gideon chased the king to the top of his tower to slay him. At this moment Noah saw an army of Lamanites approaching. He "cried out in the anguish of his soul, saying: Gideon, spare me, for the Lamanites are upon us, and they will destroy us; yea, they will destroy my people." We are then given an important piece of information about the Noahs of our lives: "Now the king was not so much concerned about his people as he was about his own life." (Mosiah 19:7–8.)

Gideon spared Noah, who then ordered the people to flee before the Lamanites. Let us suppose we are one of those who are fleeing the Lamanites. We are so used to following our king that we grab our family and begin to run. Some members of our family would have trouble running fast enough to avoid the advancing Lamanites. The older members would also be in danger of capture or death. Fearful of being overtaken, we encourage the family to hurry, but the Lamanites are gaining on us. At this moment our leader, the man we have followed and justified and defended, gives us a new order.

"The king commanded them that all the men should leave their wives and their children, and flee before the Lamanites." (Mosiah 19:11.) Some would not do this, but in our moment of crisis, we drop the hands of our family members, abandon them to their fate, and follow our leader just as we have followed him in the past. We run, constantly looking behind to see if the Lamanites are gaining on us. Finally we realize that we have escaped. Now comes the "Noah moment."

In a clearing in the wilderness, we stop. For a moment, out of breath from running, we rest. Then the realization of what we have done strikes us. "Oh, what have I done!" we say. Suddenly all eyes begin to turn in the same direction. We all stare at Noah. For the first time we see him as he really is. He has not changed at all from what he always was, but now the blindness is gone. Earlier we had placed great *value* on this man and his priests. How much do we value him now? The full irony of Abinadi's words now comes home. His life is now "valued as a garment in a hot furnace" by the very people who once defended him. In anguish and anger at what has occurred, we burn Noah, just as we allowed the burning of Abinadi earlier.

"Noah moments" can be extremely painful. For many young women who came into my office to confess the loss of virtue, they realized what they had given up to keep the affection of a boyfriend, or should we say a boy Noah. For the young woman in my wife's Laurel class, it may come when she realizes she is addicted to a life-destroying drug. To the young man who gave in to the influences of his friends, it came when his past actions denied him the opportunity of serving a mission. We must learn to distinguish between the Noahs and the Abinadis of our lives, lest these painful moments come too late.

BEFORE IT WAS TOO LATE

Sometimes the blindness is healed before great harm is done. One evening after I related this powerful story in an institute class, a young woman who had a beautiful singing voice approached me to share her own "Noah moment."

"I got caught up in rock music," she said. "My parents were greatly distressed that I was using my talents, which they had helped me develop through music lessons, with music they felt was harmful. However, I thought they were just old-fashioned and were condemning something they knew nothing about. I joined a rock band. Even though I was uncomfortable at first with the environments we sang in and the clothing I was asked to wear, in time I adjusted and felt fine.

"Everyone but me could tell how much I was changing, but I convinced myself that the clothing was just a costume and that the lyrics were only words. I really liked a group who produced some very hard music. I had placed posters of their lead singer all over my room, much to the despair of my mother in particular. One night after a concert, I came home, turned the light on in my room, and stared at the poster of my favorite rock singer. He had on a pair of black leather pants. He was chained as if he were a prisoner with a look of pain on his face. Suddenly, I felt as if the Savior entered my room, stood beside me, and looked at the poster with me. I think the Lord gave me a great gift, because I felt so ashamed. There was nothing desirable in the poster. I saw the whole rock industry for what it was. I tore down the poster, removed all other signs of rock from my room, and put up an old picture of the Savior I'd had when I was a Mia Maid. I had a 'Noah moment' before it was too late."

Perhaps the most devastating "Noah moment" of all will be the one the wicked will face when they see the adversary and realize they have been deceived. This moment has been described in scripture. Samuel the Lamanite spoke of it in these terms: "We are surrounded by demons, yea, we are encircled about by the angels of him who hath sought to destroy our souls." (Helaman 13:37.)

The great lesson of Korihor ended with Mormon's familiar conclusion: "And thus we see that the devil will not support his children at the last day, but doth speedily drag them down to hell." (Alma 30:60.)

Enoch saw the Lord weep over those who would be destroyed in the flood. He also saw the adversary's reaction:

"He beheld Satan; and he had a great chain in his hand, and it veiled the whole face of the earth with darkness; and he looked up and laughed, and his angels rejoiced." (Moses 7:26.) So that this most tragic of "Noah moments" does not overtake us or those we love, let us diligently try to recognize the Noahs of life while we learn to trust the vision of our Abinadis.

CHAPTER EIGHT

LISTEN TO THE "WILD MEN"

The Lord knew from the very beginning that Lucifer would use numerous types of blindness to deceive mankind. Lucifer is introduced as "the father of all lies, to deceive and to *blind* men, and to lead them captive at his will." (Moses 4:4.) The Lord also knew that people in general have "eyes [that] cannot see afar off." (Moses 6:27.) In his concern for this spiritual nearsightedness, he provided for his children seers who could "see afar off." The word *seer* is better understood if we spell it fully—*see-er*. A seer is one who sees. The word *revelator* is associated with *seer*. A revelator is one who reveals. What does he reveal? He reveals what he sees.

THE WATCHMAN ON THE TOWER

For this reason the prophets, seers, and revelators of the Church are called by the scriptures the "watchman upon the tower." (D&C 101:45; see also Ezekiel 3:17.) From their higher vantage point, they can see "the enemy while he [is] yet *afar off*" so that we can prepare against him. (D&C 101:54.) The Book of Mormon describes some of the things that seers can perceive:

"A seer can know of things which are past, and also of things which are to come, and by them shall all things be revealed, . . . things . . . which otherwise could not be known. . . . Thus God has provided a means that man, through faith, might work mighty miracles; *therefore he becometh a great benefit to his fellow beings.*" (Mosiah 8:17–18.) Seers can draw from the past the lessons necessary to apply to the problems of today. They can look into the future and see how we can best prepare for challenges yet to come. Sometimes, however, we who are sitting in the trenches at the foot of the watchman's tower, and can't see as far off as the seer can, may question his vision: "What is the matter with the vision of the seer?" we may ask each other. "I can't see any enemy coming. Something must be wrong with his eyesight."

THE VISION OF LATTER-DAY SEERS

I grew up in the '50s under the leadership of President David O. McKay, who was probably best known for his teachings on the family. All prophets emphasize the family, but President McKay brought an urgency to our focus on family home evening, strong marriages, and healthy parent-and-child relationships. His best-known statement is "No other success can compensate for failure in the home." (In Conference Reports April 1935, p. 116; April 1964, p. 5.) This message he taught as early as 1935.

However, during the decade of the '50s and even into the early '60s, the societal pressures on the home and family were minor, especially compared to today. This was the age of *Father Knows Best* and *Leave It to Beaver.* Almost everything I saw on television or at the movie theater supported my family's value system. Since attacks against the stability of the home were minimal, why did President McKay place such an emphasis on family issues? He had eyes that could see afar off. He was laying defensive preparations for the all-out war against the family that would begin vigorously in the middle and late '60s and continue through today.

Part of President McKay's encouragement to families was probably based on the impact it would have on children raised during those times. If their parents followed the counsel to hold family home evenings, for example, the children would be in the habit of having them and would have a testimony of their importance. I hold family home evenings, family scripture reading, and family prayer largely because I was raised in a home where these things were standard.

President McKay was not the first to teach the importance of these things. President Joseph F. Smith gave them great emphasis even earlier. During his administration, three critical programs were started—home evening, seminary, and Scouting. These are all critical programs today in fortifying youth and helping families. He, too, had eyes that see afar off.

When President Spencer W. Kimball led the Church, he often said: "Lengthen your stride and quicken your pace." (*Ensign*, May 1978, p. 80.) He placed a strong emphasis on getting more missionaries into the field. "Every worthy young man should fill a mission," he exhorted us. (*Ensign*, October 1974, p. 14; *Ensign*, October 1977, p. 3.) In response to his encouragement, the number of missionaries began to grow. In the late '80s, remarkable events began to take place in the Soviet Union. Almost overnight the Iron Curtain countries opened for the preaching of the gospel, as did nations in Africa. President Kimball had the Church ready for the wonderful opportunities these events offered.

Why don't seers move with the times? Because they are ahead of the times. They often disagree with the temporal view because they have seen an eternal one. We will be warned, counseled, and made ready both as a Church and as individual families to the extent that we heed the seers. Whenever a seer offers counsel, our first question should be, "I wonder what he sees that is causing him to speak these words?" When President Gordon B. Hinckley, with the rest of the First Presidency and the Quorum of the Twelve Apostles (fifteen seers in unity), issued the Proclamation on the Family, I wonder what they saw that moved them to give us such a clear and strong understanding of doctrine. I am convinced that in a few years we will realize even more fully than we do now its prophetic power of preparation.

WASHING AWAY THE WORLD

In the scriptures, the Lord teaches us the reason that a seer's vision is so sharp, and He teaches it in an unusual way. When Enoch was first called by the Lord, he was told, "Anoint thine eyes with clay, and wash them, and *thou shalt see*. And he did so. . . . He beheld things which were *not visible to the natural eye;* and from thenceforth came the saying abroad in the land: A seer hath the Lord raised up unto his people." (Moses 6:35–36.)

Why would the Lord desire Enoch to put clay on his eyes? Surely the clay was meant to represent the things of the world. Seers can see so much more clearly and distantly because they have washed the things of the world from their eyes. They do not see with the eyes of political correctness, or popularity, or self-aggrandizement, for these are things of the earth. The "natural eye" sees with these considerations, but a prophet must be above such influences. He understands, as Paul taught, that "the *natural man* receiveth not the things of the Spirit of God: for they are foolishness unto him: neither can he know them, because they are spiritually discerned." (1 Corinthians 2:14.) Seers also understand, as King Benjamin taught, that "the *natural man* is an enemy to God." (Mosiah 3:19.) As the book of Daniel tells us, the seers can help us "dissolve doubts" (Daniel 5:16) regarding the social, scientific, political, ethical, and moral issues of the modern world.

LISTENING TO THE "WILD MEN"

As Enoch began to challenge the standards, beliefs, and behaviors of his time, "all men were offended because of him." (Moses 6:37.) This is often the lonely road a seer must walk. Interestingly, everyone came to hear Enoch preach anyway. "We go yonder," they said, "to behold the seer, for he prophesieth, and there is a strange thing in the land; a *wild man* hath come among us." (Moses 6:38.) In what way is a seer a "wild man"? Some of the earlier prophets, like Elijah and John the Baptist, are portrayed as living in the desert like wild men, but I think there is another reason.

I believe the Lord wants his prophets to be "wild." They are untamed, uncontrolled, not corralled or fenced in by the standards or thought patterns of men. In the hands of the Lord they are tame, but they are not controlled by men. Most people like "tame" prophets—those who tell them what they want to hear. They want soothsayers who will tell them soothing things. As Isaiah said, "This is a rebellious people . . . which say to the seers, See not; and to the prophets, Prophesy not unto us right things, speak unto us smooth things, prophesy deceits: Get you out of the way, turn aside out of the path, cause the Holy One of Israel to cease from before us." (Isaiah 30:9–11.) Most people want to control their prophets, to limit their words to certain topics. However, the Lord's seers may speak or offer counsel on any subject, at any time, and in any setting. A great mist-clearing voice encourages us, "Listen to the wild men!"

THE FACE OF A PROPHET

The scriptures teach us both directly and indirectly the power of a prophet in dispersing the darkness Satan sends to blind our eyes. The fifth chapter of Helaman recounts the story of Nephi and Lehi, who were bound in prison, awaiting their execution. When the Lamanites came to take their lives, they were "encircled about with a pillar of fire." At the same time, the Lamanites "were overshadowed with a cloud of darkness, and an awful solemn fear came upon them." (Helaman 5:24, 28.) This cloud of darkness represents their spiritual state. The Lord was showing them an outward manifestation of their spiritual state. We are told that "they could not flee because of the cloud of darkness." (Helaman 5:34.) There was, however, something powerful enough to penetrate the darkness and show them the way.

"[Aminadab] turned him about, and behold, *he saw through the cloud of darkness the faces of Nephi and Lehi;* and behold, they did shine exceedingly." Aminadab cried to the others trapped in the darkness, encouraging them to look to the one source of light visible to them. "And behold, there was power given unto them that they did turn and look; and *they did behold the faces of Nephi and Lehi.*" (Helaman 5:36–37.)

When the adversary sends his clouds of darkness, his temptations, his deceptions and deceits, we need only look to the faces of the prophets. Their light is strong enough to penetrate whatever clouds may come our way. But just as the Lamanites had to turn and look, so we must turn and look. The light is there if we desire it. If we seek it, wonderful promises are offered.

"WHITE AS THE COUNTENANCE OF JESUS"

In a similar manner, the Savior visually taught the Nephites and Lamanites the power of His newly chosen disciples. He asked the disciples to pray. While they were praying, "Jesus blessed them . . . and his countenance did smile upon them, and the light of his countenance did shine upon them, and behold *they were as white as the countenance and also the garments of Jesus;* and behold the whiteness thereof did exceed all the whiteness, yea, even there could be nothing upon earth so white as the whiteness thereof." (3 Nephi 19:25.) Two times

Jesus gave the people this manifestation of apostolic approval. (See v. 30.) If a similar experience took place during general conference, and we looked up to see the apostles praying with the Savior standing next to them, smiling, and they radiated the same beautiful white light as the Savior, what a lesson we would receive from that sight!

DISPERSING THE POWERS
OF DARKNESS

On the day the Church was organized, April 6, 1830, the Lord offered one revelation. Given the importance of the day, this revelation has added significance. On that day the Lord gave His new church a commandment, stated in the plainest terms, so we could not fail to recognize how important the words were to the Church:

"*Thou shalt give heed* unto all [the prophet's] *words* and *commandments* which he shall give unto you as he receiveth them, walking in all holiness before me; for his word ye shall receive, as if from mine own mouth, in all patience and faith." (D&C 21:4–5.) Notice that we are to listen to both the words and the commandments of the prophet. As the Lord stated, it is not good for Him to "command in all things." (D&C 58:26.) Many times the prophets give counsel rather than commandments. But we are to heed both their words and their commandments.

We must do this "in all patience and faith." Sometimes it takes patience to see the wisdom of the seers. As we have already discussed, they are ahead of their times; but if we will be patient and have faith, eventually we will see the value of their words and their counsel.

The Lord promises three things that will happen as a result of our obedience, faith, and patience. "By doing these things the gates of hell shall not prevail against you; yea, and the Lord God *will disperse the powers of darkness from before you*, and cause the heavens to shake for your good and his name's glory." (D&C 21:6.) "Shake" in this context means to overflow. The heavens will pour out good things upon us. These blessings are ours to receive if we will do what the Lord asks us.

CLOSING THE EYES OF THE SEERS

Since prophets can disperse the clouds of darkness with their light, Satan must employ tactics that cause people to dismiss or ignore the seer's vision. This he does in a number of ways. When Abinadi's message became too painful for Noah to hear, Noah cried out, "Away with this fellow, and slay him; for what have we to do with him, for he is mad." (Mosiah 13:1.) If you don't like the message, attack the messenger. No one needs to listen to a madman, hence Noah could ignore the words of Abinadi. Today some dismiss the prophet's message by claiming that he is too old, too conservative, or uneducated on a specific topic. Some say that he doesn't understand their needs or situation. Others comfort themselves with the thought that they are the unique exception to the general rule. Some play the words of one prophet against those of another or one scripture against another, "wresting" its meaning. When Stephen's message began to prick the consciences of his hearers, they "stopped their ears." (Acts 7:57.) Some simply refuse to listen. Some listen, but as Ezekiel teaches, "Thou art unto them as a very lovely song of one that hath a pleasant voice, . . . for they hear thy words, but they do them not." (Ezekiel 33:32.) Some use doubt as a permanent defense: "Since I do not really know the Church is true and led by prophets, I am not obligated to heed them," they reason. The trouble is, they will not try to obtain the testimony they need.

Some, as Jeremiah discovered, ask for counsel, anticipating that it will match their own thoughts; when it does not, they refuse to believe that the Lord really spoke through the prophet. "Ye dissembled in your hearts," Jeremiah told them, "when ye sent me unto the Lord your God, saying, Pray for us unto the Lord our God; and according unto all that the Lord our God shall say, so declare unto us, and we will do it. And now I have this day declared it to you; but ye have not obeyed the voice of the Lord your God, nor any thing for the which he hath sent me unto you." (Jeremiah 42:20–21.)

All of these methods may succeed in fulfilling Isaiah's prophecy about the latter days—a prophecy we pray may never include us in its fulfillment: "The Lord hath poured out upon you the spirit of deep sleep, and hath closed your eyes: the prophets and your rulers, the seers hath he covered." (Isaiah 29:10.)

PURE INTELLIGENCE

When I was a deacon in southern California, my mother told me that Elder William J. Critchlow was coming to speak at our stake conference. I remember that conference. We were late. We sat on the stage far from the podium. I could not see the speakers. When Elder Critchlow stood to speak, I wanted to see him. My mother told me to take a folding chair and carry it up the aisle, place it in front of the podium, and listen to "one of God's servants." I did so. As I think back on it, it must have looked rather strange to Brother Critchlow and the audience. There was a twelve-year-old boy in the middle of the aisle, staring straight up at the podium. I don't remember much of what he said, but a spirit settled over me as he talked, a spirit that whispered, "This is a man of God; you may believe him." When he was finished and the meeting was over, he came up to me and laid his hand on my shoulder; I felt the assurance of pure intelligence.

As a nineteen-year-old missionary in Lyon, France, I was told that Elder Boyd K. Packer was coming to a zone conference. All the missionaries were waiting in the meetinghouse for him. I was conversing with my companion with my back to the door when Elder Packer entered. Even without seeing him, I felt him enter the room. I felt the influence of pure testimony and pure intelligence as it came from him. I knew that he was a chosen servant of God, one of the noble and great ones. He shook my hand, and I felt the same assurance I did as a boy staring up at the pulpit during stake conference. It wouldn't have mattered which apostle came into the room; the feeling would have been the same.

Seers, past and present, send their light into the darkest mists. There is no mist thick enough to totally obscure their influence. Our children are taught this in Primary when they sing, "Follow the prophet, follow the prophet, follow the prophet, he knows the way." May that truth guide us through the mists of our times and home to our Father in Heaven.

CHAPTER NINE

DON'T LEAP WITH
THE SHEEP

One summer when a bunch of us boys had taken a day off from the chores of the ranch to look for Indian arrowheads, we came across six lambs out on the desert. The lambs had strayed from their flock, I suppose, for they had no owner's mark on their wool. They were wild, and roughly a year old. We decided to try to catch them and take them back to the ranch. We spread out over the desert and attempted to box them in, but they were resistant to the idea of being tamed.

For over an hour we ran around, making grabs for them as they broke through our tightening circle. After many unsuccessful attempts, we got an idea. There were many cliffs in the area, so we thought we would back them against the edge of a cliff, thus blocking off their escape. We were closing in on them when the biggest one turned and ran for the edge of the cliff. To our amazement, instead of stopping he leaped over the edge and plunged to his death. We backed off when we saw this, to give the remaining lambs some room, but to our shock the other five raced toward the cliff. One by one all five of them jumped to their deaths. I had heard of sheep doing strange things like this, but I would never have believed it if I hadn't seen it myself.

FOLLOWING THE HERD

In spite of all our talk about individualism and doing our own thing, mankind seems to have a built-in herd instinct. This can work for us or against us, depending on which way the herd is moving. Unfortunately, most of the herd in the modern world is jumping over a moral cliff. The power of peer pressure is a tremendous mist that has blinded old and young alike for centuries. It is a particularly effective mist today. Part of its usefulness for Satan is found in its economy. If he can get the lead sheep to leap, the others often follow without thinking. Too many people never clearly reason out their positions on fashions, music, morality, politics, or even religion. Like the Israelites in the land of Canaan, they simply accept the standards "of the people that were round about them." (Judges 2:12.)

The scriptures provide advice on how to clear this mist and marvelous examples of those who would not jump with the other sheep. Because this is such an important defense to develop, examples are found in every book of scripture. Three powerful ones come to mind.

"WHAT DO YE SAY?"

During the ministry of the Savior, He withdrew to the coasts of Caesarea Philippi to be alone with His disciples. When He had found the needed seclusion, He asked them a question: "Whom *do men say* that I the Son of man am?" This first question was answered by the disciples as they related to the Lord some of the prevailing theories of the day: "Some say that thou art John the Baptist: some, Elias; and others, Jeremias, or one of the prophets." (Matthew 16:13–14.)

The Lord then posed a second question: "But whom *say ye* that I am?" (Matthew 16:15.) I have pondered why Jesus asked that first question when the second one was the critical one for the disciples. I believe the first question sets the stage for the second one and is, therefore, very important. The Savior is teaching us that what men say must not be the crucial factor in our lives. What do *we* say? What do *we* think? Perhaps more important, we need to ask ourselves what is the source of our opinions, thoughts, beliefs, and actions.

Peter answered the second question boldly and with conviction: "Thou art the Christ, the Son of the living God." Jesus' response to this testimony is highly instructive: "Blessed art thou, Simon Bar-jona: for *flesh and blood hath not revealed it unto thee, but my Father which is in heaven*." (Matthew 16:16–17.)

More important even than our own thoughts on any issue is our Father in Heaven's view on the matter, so we might add a third question: "What does my Father in Heaven say?" It does not matter what men say, for their opinions are often wrong. But it does matter what we say, and whether we are getting our beliefs from the world or from God.

The Savior continued His instruction by assuring Peter, "Upon this rock I will build my church; and the gates of hell shall not prevail against it." (Matthew 16:18.) The Church's foundation, as well as our own, must be built upon what the Father reveals, not upon the direction the world is traveling; but there are always forces that try to bend the Church as an institution or its individual members to follow the flow of the times, to consider too deeply what men say. This we cannot allow to happen. The Savior's promise to us as families, as individuals, and to the Church at large is the assurance that "the gates of hell shall not prevail" if we follow the Father.

THE WILL OF THE FATHER

Jesus is the greatest example of this principle. The "gates of hell" never troubled Him in the tiniest matter. He was never lost in a mist. The main reason this is so was His complete reliance upon the Father's will.

It is interesting to study introductions. When I speak, I am frequently asked how I would like to be introduced. We can tell a lot about people by their answer to that question, for it tends to reveal what they consider most important about themselves. How did Jesus introduce himself? A few examples may be instructive. When He appeared to the Nephites He said, "I have drunk out of that bitter cup which the Father hath given me, and have glorified the Father in taking upon me the sins of the world, in the which *I have suffered the will of the Father in all things from the beginning.*" (3 Nephi 11:11.)

Three times He mentioned His Father. During His ministry among the Nephites, Jesus mentioned the Father more than 150 times. On a later visit to the disciples, Jesus introduced His definition of the gospel with these words: "This is the gospel which I have given unto you—that I *came into the world to do the will of my Father, because my Father sent me.*" (3 Nephi 27:13.) In section 19 of the Doctrine and Covenants, Jesus introduces himself by saying, "I, having accomplished and finished *the will of him whose I am,* even the Father, concerning me— . . . retaining all power, even to the destroying of Satan and his works at the end of the world." (D&C 19:2–3.) Here the suggestion is made that Satan will be destroyed because Jesus followed the Father's will in all things. Jesus would never have said, "I am my own man." He was His Father's man, and He knew that the ability to accomplish His calling rested upon the rock of His Father's will.

BOW TO THE WORLD OR WALK WITH THE SAVIOR

The second example of refusing to bend to the instincts of the herd is found in the book of Daniel. Nebuchadnezzar, the king of Babylon, made a great image of gold, then gathered all his officers and rulers together with the people to its dedication. "Then an herald cried aloud, To you it is commanded, O people, nations, and languages, that at what time ye hear the sound of . . . all kinds of musick, ye fall down and worship the golden image that Nebuchadnezzar the king hath set up." (Daniel 3:4–5.) The punishment for not bowing down was death in the fiery furnace.

The people gathered, and when the music sounded, they all fell down to worship except three young Hebrew men— Hananiah, Mishael, and Azariah. (With all things considered, I wonder if they would not prefer that we use their Hebrew names.) They were hauled before the king, who gave them a second chance to bow before the image of Babylon, accompanied with a warning about the fiery furnace: "Who is that god that shall deliver you out of my hand?" he asked them. (Daniel 3:15.)

How often we hear the music of Babylon calling us to worship and bow before the images of the world, both literally and figuratively. (Modern music is so often wrapped up in the images of the world.) In our imagination we can see those three young men standing amid the kneeling multitudes, alone and conspicuous. "We are not careful to answer thee in this matter," they told the king. In other words, we are not going to be politically correct and go with the flow or say what you want to hear. "If it be so, our God whom we serve is able to deliver us from the burning fiery furnace. . . . But if not, be it known unto thee, O king, that we will not serve thy gods, nor worship the golden image which thou hast set up." (Daniel 3:16–17.)

The results of this decision are well known. They were thrown into the furnace, but the expectations of the king failed. "Lo, I see four men loose, walking in the midst of the fire," he said, "and they have no hurt; and the form of the fourth is like the Son of God." (Daniel 3:25.) Simply spoken, the message of this story could be stated like this: "If you refuse to bow to the images of the world, you may walk with the Savior."

IN THE LIKENESS OF THE WORLD

There are two interesting allusions to this story as it relates to the latter days. In the Lord's preface to the Doctrine and Covenants, he said, "They seek not the Lord to establish his righteousness, but every man walketh in his own way, and after the *image of his own god, whose image is in the likeness of the world,* and whose substance is that of an idol, which waxeth old and shall perish in Babylon, even Babylon the great, which shall fall." (D&C 1:16.)

Early in the Restoration the Lord mentioned one of the mists we would have to confront. We would be tempted to bow to the images of the world. They are powerful and often more immediate in their compulsion than the interests of Zion. We may not believe in the images of Babylon, but it is so much easier to kneel than to stand alone amid the stares of the bowing masses. The Lord encourages us, however. The images of the world will fall. They cannot last. We do not have to live very long to see how transitory these images can be.

The second allusion is found in the book of Revelation. It is a subtle allusion, easy to miss unless we read carefully. In the thirteenth chapter, John describes a great beast that will arise in the latter days. In the footnote, Joseph Smith tells us that this great beast is "in the likeness of the kingdoms of the earth." (JST, Revelation 13:1.) A command is given "to them that dwell on the earth, that they should *make an image to the beast* . . . and cause that as many as would not worship the image of the beast should be killed." (Revelation 13:14–15.)

There is much speculation about the fulfillment of this prophecy that we will not discuss here. I would caution us not to read it too literally. It is not difficult, however, to catch the allusion John is making to the book of Daniel. Since all of

Revelation 13 finds its roots in Daniel, we must look there for clarification. If we have ears to hear, we will understand the hope and encouragement John is giving to those who will live in a world that worships the images of Babylon. We must not bow. Though the threat is issued that those who refuse will be killed or not allowed to "buy and sell," if we remember Hananiah, Mishael, and Azariah, we know that Someone will be walking by our side, even in the midst of a furnace of public scorn and persecution.

FIRM AND UNDAUNTED

It is often difficult to stand when others bow or to say what you think or what the Father has revealed, instead of what men say, but it is critical for the Church that we hold firm. The mist of leaping with the sheep, though thick, can be penetrated. In the Book of Mormon, the 2,060 stripling warriors provide a powerful example for youth of what can happen when they act like warriors and not like sheep.

In the midst of a critical battle, Helaman wrote, "as the remainder of our army were about to give way before the Lamanites, behold, those two thousand and sixty were firm and undaunted." (Alma 57:20.) A common excuse for breaking the commandments or going against the counsel of the Lord is, "Everyone else is doing it." There is an almost certain assurance when we hear those words that Satan is spreading a mist before us. The stripling warriors would not give way even though all the rest of the army was about to do so. So too must young people refuse to give way even when everyone else is heading for the cliff. The landing at the bottom is not softened by the knowledge that so many other sheep fell with us. Our standing firm, as is discussed in greater detail in another chapter, may save others.

The firmness of these young men came from two primary sources—the testimony of their parents, particularly of their mothers, and their choice of a prophet, Helaman, to lead them. Notice also how they followed that prophet-leader: "They did obey and observe to perform *every word of command with exactness.*" (Alma 57:21.) We are told that all of the 2,060 were wounded in the battles. Undoubtedly some wounds will be suffered in the battle against the forces of Babylon, but they need not overcome us if we "stand fast in that liberty wherewith God has made [us] free; and . . . are *strict* to remember the Lord [our] God from day to day; yea, [and] observe to keep [God's] statutes, and his judgments . . . continually." (Alma 58:40.) The word *strict* is not particularly popular today. Sadly, too many feel like the people living during Alma the Younger's days: "They began to be offended because of the *strictness* of the word." (Alma 35:15.) If we will take inspiration from the example of these 2,060 young men who followed Helaman, by standing fast when others give way, none will die in the spiritual battles of today, as none died in their war against the Lamanites.

COMMON CONSENT

As is true of most of Satan's mists, leaping with the sheep is a corruption of a true principle of heaven. That principle is known in the Church today as common consent. In an early section of the Doctrine and Covenants, the Lord revealed to Joseph Smith this wise law: "All things shall be done by common consent in the church, by much prayer and faith, for all things you shall receive by faith." (D&C 26:2.) Plainly put, this law states: if the sheep are following the Savior, go with them. The scriptures are filled with messages suggesting that we are the Lord's flock and should behave like sheep in following our Shepherd.

A short time after the law of common consent was revealed to Joseph Smith, a small crisis threatened the Church. Hiram Page, one of the Eight Witnesses to the Book of Mormon, "had a certain stone, and professed to be receiving revelations by its aid concerning the upbuilding of Zion and the order of the Church. Several members had been deceived by these claims." (D&C 28: heading.)

After instructing Oliver Cowdery to correct Hiram Page, the Lord said, "All things must be done in order, and by common consent in the church, by the prayer of faith." (D&C 28:13.) When mists of deception threaten, we are to trust the common beliefs, practices, and wisdom of the combined membership of the Church. We should remember Mosiah taught his people: "It is not common that the voice of the people desireth anything contrary to that which is right." (Mosiah 29:26.) Common consent means more than raising our hands to sustain leaders in their callings; that is only its most outward manifestation. It also shows that we trust the Saints as a body in many other issues.

TRUST THE COMMON WISDOM

When students have posed questions about a practice or doctrine that is out of balance with the truth, I often ask them, "What do 11 million members of the Church feel about this issue?" In almost every instance you may trust that common wisdom.

A bishop wanted to choose the counselors for his auxiliary leaders, which caused great frustration for the Relief Society, Young Women, and Primary presidents. It would be a simple matter to ask him, "What are 12,000 other bishops throughout the Church doing? Are they choosing the counselors, or are they allowing the presidents to seek the inspiration in company with them?"

A sister once felt she should pray to the Savior, quoting a few scriptures to substantiate her point. "To whom are the other hundreds of members of your ward and thousands of members of your stake praying to?" I asked her. Another felt that the Second Coming was very near and that it was time to sell her house and move from the city to a small town where she felt she would be safe. "Are tens of thousands of Saints selling their houses and moving to the country?" I asked.

As a people, we have the united counsel of fifteen prophets, seers, and revelators to guide us. We have the examples and truths of the scriptures. We have the inspiration and whisperings of the Holy Ghost. We also have the combined wisdom and consent of millions of other members who desire to follow the Good Shepherd. If we belong to the flock of the Good Shepherd, we may leap with the sheep, for we know it will be a leap of faith, a leap through the mists of darkness into the light of God's love.

CHAPTER TEN

AVOIDING DELILAH'S BARBER SHOP

W e learn another powerful les-
son from the 2,060 young Lamanite warriors that can be
augmented by examining the story of Samson in the Old Testament. One of the first things Mormon recorded about the
stripling warriors indicates a source of their strength: "They
entered into a covenant . . . ; yea, even they *covenanted* that they
never would give up their liberty, but they would fight *in all
cases* to protect the Nephites and themselves from *bondage.*"
(Alma 53:17.) Covenants can exert a powerful influence to
keep us separate from the world. That is one of their main func-
tions. Spiritually speaking, they allow us to keep our liberty and
avoid the bondage of the tempter, who is portrayed as holding
"a great chain in his hand." (Moses 7:26.) I call this mist-
clearing principle "staying away from the barber."

A COVENANT OF SEPARATION

The whole tragedy of Samson was recorded to illustrate the
protective power of covenants. The children of Israel were a
covenant people. That covenant relationship with God
required that they remain a separate, distinct, and holy people.

The very nature of their covenants, had they obeyed them, would have prevented any sorrowful leaps with the worldly sheep of Canaan. Simply keeping his covenants would have kept Samson from Delilah's razor. However, the Lord gave him additional help. The Lord, knowing the propensity of Samson to gravitate to the things of the world, tried to insulate him even further to help him fulfill his calling of liberating the Israelites from Philistine domination. He made him a Nazarite from his birth. Unfortunately, the liberator would in time become the captive. Those who took the vow of a Nazarite entered into an even deeper covenant relationship with God. The covenant was essentially one of separation. In Numbers, chapter 6, where the Lord describes the Nazarite covenant, the word *separation* or *separate* is used fourteen times. Nazarites promised to avoid using certain substances; for example, they were to "eat nothing that is made of the vine tree," and they were to "come at no dead body." (Numbers 6:4, 6.) As an outward sign that they had made special vows dedicating themselves to the service of God, they were not to cut their hair during the time of their separation. In essence, the length of the hair symbolized time. When the time of separation was over, the hair was cut and offered on the altar, signifying the time that had been consecrated to the Lord. In the case of Samson, his hair, representing his covenant, was the source of his strength. The message for us is clear: Covenants are the source of our strength.

TO BLIND AND BIND

Each story related about Samson details the breaking of his covenants. He married a Philistine, for example. However, as long as he maintained even one element of his covenant, his hair, the Lord chose to honor him, and his strength remained. When the Philistines learned that he loved Delilah, they "came up unto her, and said unto her, *Entice him,* and see *wherein his great strength lieth,* and by what means we may prevail against him, that we *may bind him* to afflict him." (Judges 16:5.) Notice how the words of the Philistine lords correspond so perfectly to what the adversary seeks to do.

Delilah finally prevailed, and Samson revealed the source of his strength: "I have been a Nazarite unto God from my mother's womb: if I be shaven, then my strength will go from me, *and I shall become weak, and be like any other man.*" (Judges 16:17.) The hair was not the real issue; faithfulness to his covenant was the critical factor. It kept him separate, at least in one point, from the Philistine world that was so alluring to him. It gave him strength. With the covenant in force, he was not "like any other man." So it is with us. Our covenants make us strong. They prevent the adversary, or any debilitating habit of the world, from binding us. We must stay away from Delilah's barber shop—those forces or individuals that ask us to compromise, ignore, or break our covenants. We are not like any other people. We are a holy nation.

With the last remnants of Samson's covenant gone, Delilah "began to afflict him, and his strength went from him." Unaware that he was no longer different, Samson said, "I will go out as at other times before, and shake myself. And he *wist not that the Lord was departed from him.*" (Judges 16:19–20.) When we violate our covenants, we may not realize that we have lost the Spirit, but a source of strength is gone, and we become vulnerable to the power of the adversary. This is plainly taught to us when we make sacred covenants in the temple.

The two major objectives of Lucifer as they are spoken of in the scriptures are to blind mankind and to take them captive—to shut them up in his prison. In light of these goals, the fate of Samson becomes deeply relevant in its spiritual application: "The Philistines took him, and *put out his eyes*, and brought him down to Gaza, and *bound him with fetters of brass*; and he did grind in the *prison house*." (Judges 16:21.)

BAPTISM TO SEALING

We cannot emphasize too much the strength of a covenant. It is not coincidental that "power is not given unto Satan to tempt little children, until they begin to become accountable before me." (D&C 29:47.) The adversary is not allowed to entice or challenge a child until that child is old enough to be strengthened by a covenant, the covenant of baptism, with its accompanying gift of the Holy Ghost.

As I have worked with maturing youth over the years, I have noticed that, with each new covenant, changes in their spiritual strength are apparent. This comes with priesthood covenants, but especially with those of the temple. There is a difference, for example, between a young man who has been endowed and prepares for a mission and one who has not. When young people return home from their missions, they need the next edifying covenant of sealing. When it is made, once again, it is easy to see the additional spiritual power they acquire with this last and most fulfilling covenant. Without that ordinance, their progress in spiritual strength seems to be on hold.

TEMPLE COVENANTS

The promise is made, as we make our temple covenants, that power over the adversary will accompany our faithfulness to our vows. Those covenants are instrumental in keeping us separate from the world. The world emphasizes selfishness, gratification, and building up our own individual kingdoms. The temple covenants instill in us the desire to sacrifice, to consecrate ourselves to the Lord's kingdom, and to remain chaste, modest, and pure. The world stresses rebellion in the name of liberty; the temple promises liberty through obedience. The world countenances the unholy and impure; the temple steers us away from these practices as we follow the prophets and receive only those principles that are virtuous and according to the laws of the gospel. The world cleverly advertises the befuddling of our senses through the consumption of numbing substances; the temple blesses us with clarity of intellect. The world blurs the line between good and evil; the temple gives us eyes that discern the finest shades of light and dark. The world mocks the marriage relationship and casually severs the binding ties of husband and wife; the temple makes those ties eternal and shows us how to deepen relationships. The world suggests that joy comes in possessions; the temple testifies that joy comes in righteous posterity. Faithfulness to the endowment and the sealing covenants will keep us separate from the sins of our generation.

The one thing we take with us when we leave the temple, and covenant to always wear, is given as a constant reminder of the protective power of covenants. It is important that we renew them frequently. Each Sabbath the sacrament strengthens us as we ponder our baptismal promises and whose name we bear. Each visit to the Lord's house deepens our commitment and clears mists of mortality. There simply is no influence on earth that can blind and bind us as long as we *stay away from Delilah's barber shop.*

President Gordon B. Hinckley testified of covenant power while instructing the General Authorities and their wives: "We are a covenant people. I have had the feeling that if we could just encourage our people to live by three or four covenants everything else would take care of itself; we would not have to have anything else except to go forward with our program."

He then mentioned three covenants he felt were critical: the sacrament, tithing, and the temple. "If our people could only learn to live by these covenants, everything else would take care of itself, I am satisfied. We would not have to worry about sacrament meeting attendance. We would not have to worry about willingness to serve missions. We would not have to worry about divorce and the many requests for cancellation of temple sealings. We would not have to worry about any of those things." (*Teachings of Gordon B. Hinckley* [Salt Lake City: Deseret Book, 1997], pp. 146–47.)

The stripling warriors maintained their liberty because they were true to their covenant. Samson was blinded and bound by the Philistines because he was not true to his. Delilah's barber shop is still around and open for business. Let us not enter, for grinding in the prison house is the only reward a Philistine world has to offer.

CHAPTER ELEVEN

FLY YOUR TITLE
OF LIBERTY

I recall a conversation I had with a college student who had failed the biggest test of the term. In one of his classes, the professor was challenging some of the positions of the Church. They were not direct criticisms but involved mocking some things we hold dear. He was one of the few LDS students. "I just sat there," he said. "I knew the professor was wrong in what he was teaching, but I just sat there. I wanted to say something, to clarify and affirm what he was making fun of, but I just sat there." I understood his emotions, for I, too, have sometimes failed to speak up when I should have.

We are warned by the Savior: "Neither cast ye your pearls before swine, lest they trample them under their feet, and turn again and rend you." (Matthew 7:6.) At times, therefore, silence is the appropriate response, and we must keep our pearls in our pockets. But the Spirit may move us to make a stand when the circumstances merit one, and then we must be willing to fly our titles of liberty.

PRECARIOUS AND DANGEROUS TIMES

In a critical moment in Nephite history, Amalickiah threatened to destroy the freedom established by King Mosiah. His flattery had even succeeded in causing many to dissent from the Church in support of his values and plans. Mormon said of this period, "Thus were the affairs of the people of Nephi *exceedingly precarious and dangerous.*" (Alma 46:7.) Mormon then drew the conclusion, "We also see the great wickedness one very wicked man can cause to take place among the children of men." (Alma 46:9.)

If Lucifer can wreak havoc through the influence of "one very wicked man," cannot the Lord, in turn, promote great righteousness through the influence of one very good man? Amalickiah's foil at this period is Captain Moroni. Seeing the growing strength of Amalickiah, "he rent his coat; and he took a piece thereof, and wrote upon it—In memory of our God, our religion, and freedom, and our peace, our wives, and our children—and he fastened it upon the end of a pole. . . . He went forth among the people, waving the rent part of his garment in the air, *that all might see the writing which he had written,* . . . *crying* . . . Whosoever will maintain this title upon the land, *let them come forth.* . . . And . . . when Moroni had proclaimed these words, behold, *the people came running.*" (Alma 46:12, 19–21.)

Spiritually speaking, we live in a "precarious and dangerous" time also. Our values, standards, ethics, morals, and programs are often mocked, debunked, or ignored by the world. In such times it is often difficult to write our beliefs on our coats and wave them before the world, just as it was difficult for my young college friend to stand up in class. But there are times when our own personal titles of liberty must be waved if we are to survive our own precarious era.

Lucifer's mist in such times is the fear that we are alone in our beliefs. When we wave our titles, will anyone rally around us, as did Moroni's people? What if they don't come running to our support? That is the chance we must take, but defeat is assured if someone does not stand up. Often we will be surprised at how many share our values but lack the courage to wave their own titles.

SEVEN THOUSAND IN ISRAEL

Even Elijah, the great Old Testament prophet, wondered if he was alone in his beliefs. After his dramatic confrontation with the priests of Baal on Mt. Carmel, Elijah fled for his life to Mt. Horeb from the murderous designs of Jezebel. He was so discouraged that "he requested for himself that he might die." (1 Kings 19:4.) When asked by the Lord what he was doing so far away from the place of his ministry, Elijah replied, "I have been very jealous for the Lord God of hosts: for the children of Israel have forsaken thy covenant, thrown down thine altars, and slain thy prophets with the sword; *and I, even I only, am left;* and they seek my life, to take it away." (1 Kings 19:10.)

The Lord told Elijah to return to his labors with the following assurance: "I have left me seven thousand in Israel, all the knees which have not bowed unto Baal, and every mouth which hath not kissed him." (1 Kings 19:18.) Often, if the title of belief is waved, and the invitation to come forth is issued, the seven thousand will come running.

When David came to the Israelite camp, everyone was afraid of facing the Philistine champion. But after David's victory, the rest of the army was infused with courage. They rallied around David, "and the men of Israel and of Judah arose, and shouted, and pursued the Philistines." (1 Samuel 17:52.)

THEY STARTED TO APPLAUD

I remember the experience of another student in a college class. He was attending a rather liberal university in Colorado, and the class was for prospective teachers. They had been assigned to read an adolescent book and assess its worth for assigning in a junior-high-school setting. The theme of the novel was the sexual attraction and subsequent activities of two ninth graders. It was descriptive and plain in its language. This Latter-day Saint student related what happened in these words: "I sat there listening to my fellow students approve of the book. They spoke of avoiding censorship and the need to bring some things more into the open. Students were sexually active anyway. To ignore what was going on in their lives was puritanical. They would teach it in their own classes without embarrassment. These types of comments continued throughout the period. Though they were trying to be modern and sophisticated, I got the impression that they were mainly saying what they thought all the other students and the professor wanted to hear. The class knew that I was a Latter-day Saint, and I decided when the discussion started that I would say nothing, even though I was offended by the content of the novel.

"Toward the end of the period, however, I found myself raising my hand. 'I have listened for some time to the comments of my fellow students,' I said, 'and I don't wish to be judgmental, but this is simply an unacceptable, immoral novel. It has no literary value and does not belong in the schools of America. It was written to make money off the already too-excited curiosity of young people. I believe that any teacher who introduced it to his or her students would be doing them harm. In light of all the good books that could be taught, a teacher who used this one would be irresponsible in fulfilling the trust given by parents, the community, and the students.'"

This student had waved his personal title of liberty. He now waited for the criticism and abuse he was sure was about to descend. He felt alone and doubted that anyone else in the class would come running.

"There was a long pause," he continued, "and then from the corner someone started clapping. Another joined him, and then another. Soon the entire class was applauding. I was astonished by the reaction. The class ended, but many students came up to me afterward and said, 'I was thinking the same things, but was afraid everyone would feel I was out of it.'"

SHAKING THE POWERS OF HELL

We never know when we write our beliefs and standards upon our title and wave it what reaction we will receive, but as often as not, others will take courage from our stand, and the wickedness of the Amalickiahs of the world will be challenged. As a people, it is the opportunity of the Latter-day Saints to wave their titles of liberty. The power of the Church in these days is the assurance we receive from the Lord that if we are true to our beliefs and commandments, we will truly be free. We announce to the world in a clear voice where true liberty and happiness lie. We have seen the Church leaders wave their titles without hesitation. Perhaps the most dramatic recent example of this is the Proclamation on the Family.

So we would have no doubt how important taking a stand is in fighting the mists of the adversary, Mormon wrote, "If all men had been, and were, and ever would be, like unto Moroni, behold, the very powers of hell would have been shaken forever; yea, the devil would never have power over the hearts of the children of men." (Alma 48:17.)

HIDING UNDER A BUSHEL

If we are intent on doing good, Lucifer will try to prevent us from spreading that goodness. That is why Jesus told His followers they must not hide their light under a bushel but put it "on a candlestick; and it giveth light unto all that are in the house." (Matthew 5:15.)

When I was a student in junior high school, I was very fond of the Boy Scouts. Everyone knew this and one day decided to try to embarrass me. During a class they passed around a sheet of paper titled "Real Man Test." It was divided down the middle. On one side, in varying and increasing degrees of intimacy, they had listed the steps boys and girls take in their relationships. The first thing on the list was "Afraid to look at a girl." This continued through each step, including talking with a girl, holding a girl's hand, putting your arm around her, kissing her, and so on. The last step listed was a slang expression for fornication.

On the other side of the paper was the rating of manhood. Each step had a rating. Next to the last step was written, "A Real Man." However, it was the first step everyone was so excited for me to see. When the paper was slipped onto my desk, I could feel everyone's eyes on me and could hear the laughter beginning. Next to the first step was the rating "Boy Scout."

I felt my face go red as the laughter grew. At that moment I did not particularly feel like standing up and repeating the Scout oath and law. I believed in them and enjoyed Scouting, but I just wanted to pull the bushel basket over my head and let the light radiate inside alone.

From time to time in our lives, we may silently say to the Lord, "Is it not enough to love the light and live by the light? Must we also put it on display? We don't want the light to go out, Lord, but it would be so much more comfortable to let it shine under the bushel." Perhaps the Lord's reply would be a question: "What will happen to the candle of your light if it is covered with the bushel?" We all know the answer—it will go out. Knowing this, we understand why it is so important to wave our titles from time to time, why we must willingly choose to allow the light to remain, sometimes uncomfortably, radiating high upon its candlestick. These actions become a defense for us; they keep the light burning. They dispel the mists of darkness that are ever present in this mortal world.

TITLES OF CONTENTION, NOT LIBERTY

Lucifer does not give up when we rise to fly our flags. He has another mist he can employ, one that mutes the power of those who wave their titles. It is not only important that we wave our titles of liberty; it is also important how we do so. The first chapter of Alma says there were many Nephites who did not share the beliefs of those who accepted Christ. Some followed Nehor, for example, and persecution of the Christians commenced. This was not a physical persecution, but "they did persecute them, and afflict them with all manner of words." (Alma 1:20.) Many of the believers wanted to stand up for their beliefs, but they chose the wrong way to make their stands. "There were many among them who began to be proud, and began to contend warmly with their adversaries, even unto blows; yea, they would smite one another with their fists." (Alma 1:22.)

One of the first things Jesus taught the assembled Nephites and Lamanites when he appeared at Bountiful was to avoid contention: "There shall be no disputations among you, as there have hitherto been. . . . He that hath the spirit of contention is not of me, but is of the devil, who is the father of contention, and he stirreth up the hearts of men to contend with anger, one with another." (3 Nephi 11:28–29.)

THE PARROT AND MONKEY SHOW

President Joseph F. Smith learned something about the mist of contention and its ability to blind people to the righteous titles of liberty that are waving before them. In a letter to his son he shared an experience he had during a mission to England when he was a young man.

"I never but once was the cause of a disturbance. That was in Sheffield, during my first experience in speaking English. (Previous to that I had been to the Islands.) We had a large audience. William M. Gibson, a great preacher, was present, but I was speaking, and I said that 'the authority of the apostles of today was the same as that held by the apostles of Christ's day, and that the word of modern apostles was as good as the word of the ancient apostles!' Somebody in the audience cried out,

'Blasphemy!' This was too much for my boyish temper to bear.
The proposition I had made seemed so clear, so plain, and so
indisputable to my mind, I could not brook a shout of
'Blasphemy,' and let loose on my opponent upon apostate
Christianity, hireling ministers and upon those opposed to the
truth in general, in my best licks, and by the time I got through,
I had stirred up the emissaries of his Satanic Majesty until they
were red hot, and the parrot and monkey show began in good
shape! Brother Gibson tried to quell the riot, but the excited
mob would not listen to him, would not hear any more, and
made for our stand! We slipped through the crowd and made
for home. But some of the leaders were aching to get hold of
me, and hung round for hours to get a chance. Well, this experience taught me a good lesson. Thereafter, I moderated my
fervor, became more diplomatic in the presence of a mixed
crowd, and avoided showing any temper when reviled. In fact,
I learned to be reviled without reviling back again, to take an
insult without retorting, except in meekness and gentlemanly
candor. . . . To win one's respect and confidence, approach him
mildly, kindly. No friendship was ever gained by an attack upon
principle or upon man, but by calm reason and the lowly Spirit
of Truth. If you have built for a man a better house than his
own, and he is willing to accept yours and forsake his, then, and
not till then, should you proceed to tear down the old structure.
Rotten though it may be, it will require some time for it to lose
all its charms and fond memories of its former occupant.
Therefore, let *him,* not *you,* proceed to tear it away." (Letter
from Joseph F. Smith to Hyrum M. Smith, in *From Prophet to
Son,* Smith and Kenney, comps. and eds. [Salt Lake City:
Deseret Book Co., 1981], pp. 41–43.)

CHAPTER TWELVE

WALL-WATCHERS OR GRAPE-GATHERERS

Before attempting to conquer the promised land, Moses sent twelve men, one from each tribe and "every one a ruler among them" into the land of Canaan. (Numbers 13:2.) They searched it from the north to the south. From the brook Eshcol they cut down "a branch with one cluster of grapes, and they bare it between two upon a staff; and they brought of the pomegranates, and of the figs." (Numbers 13:23.)

Returning to the main encampment, they assured the children of Israel that "the land . . . surely . . . floweth with milk and honey; and this is the fruit of it." (Numbers 13:27.) However, in spite of the wonders of the land, the spies reported that "the people be strong that dwell in the land, and the cities are *walled, and very great*. . . . We be not able to go up against the people; for they are stronger than we. And they brought up an evil report of the land." (Numbers 13:28, 31–32.)

Two of the spies, Caleb and Joshua, disagreed with the assessment of the other ten spies. They confirmed the fruitfulness of the land and testified, "Let us go up at once, and possess it; for we are well able to overcome it." (Numbers 13:30.)

Now the people had a choice. Would they direct their attention to the large cluster of grapes and the promise of future bountiful harvests, or would they concentrate on the height of the walls and the difficulties in conquering the land? Unfortunately, they chose to focus on the difficulties rather than the blessings.

Fearful, weeping all night, and lacking faith, they viewed themselves "as grasshoppers" (Numbers 13:33) compared to the might of the Canaanites, and they rebelled against Moses, Caleb, and Joshua, desiring to return to Egypt. Caleb and Joshua tried to kindle faith in their hearts by assuring them, "If the Lord delight in us, then he will bring us into this land, and give it us; a land which floweth with milk and honey. Only rebel not ye against the Lord, neither fear ye the people of the land; for they are bread for us." (Numbers 14:8–9.) Their efforts, however, evoked from the congregation only the threat to stone them.

Realizing that the present generation did not have the faith necessary to claim their inheritance in the promised land, the Lord took them at their word. They had said it would be better to die in the wilderness than attempt such a difficult task as conquering the high walls and mighty warriors. As a result of this final rebellion, the Lord declared that they would wander in the wilderness until all the older generation had died. They wandered for forty years.

CHALLENGES AS BREAD

Often in our lives we hear the conflicting reports of the spies. Then we must decide whether we will become wall-watchers or grape-gatherers. Will we focus on the difficulties in obeying a certain commandment of the Lord, or will we focus on the fruits, remembering the promises He extends to those who trust Him. Whether we are dealing with paying tithing, accepting a Church calling, serving as a full-time missionary, personal challenges in our families, or difficulties at work or at school, we simply must not let the height of the walls and the power of the warriors guarding them make us view ourselves "as grasshoppers."

If the Lord delights in us, we will have sufficient strength to conquer our fears, surmount our obstacles, and enjoy the fruits of the land. As Caleb and Joshua testified, our challenges will become "as bread" for us. Let us keep our sights on the harvest, on the large clusters of grapes that beckon us forward, and not on the walls that bar the way. Of all the older generation, only Caleb and Joshua tasted the sweetness of Israel's grapes and the red richness of her pomegranates. I have often wondered how much sweeter the fruits were to them as they recalled the challenges they had overcome to enjoy them. The high walls of Canaan far too often serve as an effectual mist that paralyzes our efforts. The Lord, understanding this, many times offers His own forms of encouragement.

"HAVE NOT I SENT THEE?"

Perhaps the strength of Joshua's and Caleb's example inspired Gideon when he was asked to accomplish a similar challenge. The Israelites were under the dominion of the Midianites when the Lord sent an angel to Gideon, addressing him as a "mighty man of valour." He then gave him his commission: "Go in this thy might, and thou shalt save Israel from the hand of the Midianites: *have not I sent thee?*" (Judges 6:12, 14.)

However, Gideon did not particularly feel like a "mighty man of valour." "Oh my Lord, wherewith shall I save Israel?" he asked. "Behold, my family is poor in Manasseh, and I am the least in my father's house." (Judges 6:15.) The Lord had already answered his concerns before he expressed them. "Have not I sent thee?" he had asked. If the Lord asks us to do something, the very fact that it is requested assures us that we do have the strength and ability to accomplish it. Nephi knew this, replying to his father, "I will go and do the things which the Lord hath commanded, for I know that the Lord giveth no command-ments unto the children of men, save he shall prepare a way for them that they may accomplish the thing which he comman-deth them." (1 Nephi 3:7.) We quote this all the time, but do we deeply accept its truth?

I recall a missionary in our ward who had studied both Spanish and Russian. She was not strong in language and had once stated to her family, after working with some Chinese chil-dren, that the one language she was most grateful she would never have to learn was Mandarin. A year later, she was called on a mission to Taiwan. The wall of that language looked ever so high, and the grapes so far away. She was comforted, how-ever, by the words of the Lord to Gideon: "Have not I sent thee?" Though the study was difficult and the time for learning short, she mastered the language, and after her mission she was able to spend six months in mainland China refining her lan-guage skills while she taught English to children in a Chinese school.

The truth is, there are no walls high or thick enough to stop us. Has not the Lord sent us? I do not think it is coincidental that the first story we are told about the eventual conquest of Canaan by the younger generation is the fall of Jericho. The walls came tumbling down. The greatest fears of the earlier generation were simply unfounded. If we are willing to move forward, the Lord often removes the barriers standing between us and the rich harvest. I have often asked myself, How many walls that caused me to hesitate in the past were in reality a mirage?

THE FLEECES OF THE LORD

The Lord knows, however, that we sometimes need reassur-ances as we face our own Canaanite walls or Midianite hordes.

In his love and gentleness, he gives us "fleeces" to strengthen our resolve and comfort our shifting faith. When the moment to face the Midianites arrived, Gideon said to the Lord, "If thou wilt save Israel by mine hand, as thou hast said, Behold, I will put a fleece of wool in the floor; and if the dew be on the fleece only, and it be dry upon all the earth beside, then shall I know that thou wilt save Israel by mine hand, as thou hast said." (Judges 6:36–37.)

The next morning, Gideon "wringed the dew out of the fleece, a bowl full of water." Still needing assurance, he now asked the Lord to reverse the situation. "Let it now be dry only upon the fleece, and upon all the ground let there be dew. And God did so that night." (Judges 6:38–40.)

Some have felt that Gideon was sign-seeking—which we are warned not to do. But there is a difference between asking for a sign to *create* faith (and then deciding to act) and asking for a sign to *confirm* faith (strengthening a previous decision to act). We often say to the Lord, "Show me, and I will act." The Lord replies, "Act, and I will show you." But fleeces or not, Gideon was going to face the Midianites.

The Lord will grant us our own "fleeces" when we are in need of strength. When we cry out as did the father of the boy with a "dumb spirit," "Lord, I believe; help thou mine unbelief," the Lord is willing to respond. (Mark 9:17, 24.) When the walls look high and strong but we intend to face them anyway, the soft fleeces of comforting reassurance will come. They may come in the inspired words of a father's blessing or in a special verse of scripture we are led to in our reading. They may come as we counsel with a leader or in a conversation with a friend. Often they come with the peace of the Holy Ghost. During these times we must be careful not to let our fears blind us to the fleeces that the Lord has sent.

CHAPTER THIRTEEN

DECISIONS OF FEAR OR OF FAITH

In the scriptures there is a strong association between Satan and fear. Consider, for example, the effect of Moses' confrontation with Satan: "Moses began to fear exceedingly; and as he began to fear, he saw the bitterness of hell." (Moses 1:20.) Lucifer works by open threats as well as more subtle forms of intimidation. Since he cannot command obedience through love, respect, or honor, he compels it through fear. Fear is an effective mist, for decisions based upon fear or made under the emotion of fear are almost always disastrous. Perhaps only pride blocks the influence of the Holy Spirit more than fear. I have often wondered if the third of the hosts in heaven, who were deceived by the adversary, made their decision based upon the uncertainties of mortality. Did they fear failure or sin so much that the loss of agency seemed a small price to pay for guaranteed salvation?

"ALL THAT THY SOUL DESIRETH"

During the last years of Solomon's reign as king of Israel, he was turned from righteousness to evil by his many foreign wives. The Lord chose one of Solomon's leaders, a man named

Jeroboam, to rule over ten of the tribes of Israel upon the death of Solomon.

One day Jeroboam left Jerusalem wearing a new garment. Ahijah the prophet met him, "and they two were alone in the field: and Ahijah caught the new garment that was on him, and rent it in twelve pieces: and he said to Jeroboam, Take thee ten pieces: for *thus saith the Lord, the God of Israel,* Behold, I will rend the kingdom out of the hand of Solomon, and will give ten tribes to thee." (1 Kings 11:29–31.)

Ahijah made further promises to Jeroboam in the name of the Lord: "And I will take thee, and thou shalt reign *according to all that thy soul desireth.* . . . And it shall be, if thou wilt hearken unto all that I command thee, and wilt walk in my ways, and do that is right in my sight, to keep my statutes and my commandments . . . that *I will be with thee, and build thee a sure house.*" (1 Kings 11:37–38.)

Notice the main promises the Lord made to Jeroboam. As king of the new nation of Israel, consisting of ten of the twelve tribes, Jeroboam was to have all that his soul desired and a "sure" house—meaning that his descendants would always sit upon the throne of the ten tribes. It must be remembered, however, as in all promises of the Lord, that the blessings are conditional upon continued faithfulness and obedience. What did Jeroboam have to fear with such promises?

MOLDING CALVES OF GOLD

In time Solomon died, there was a revolt against his son Rehoboam, and, true to Ahijah's words, Jeroboam was chosen as king over the northern ten tribes. Had he stayed true to the Lord as Ahijah counseled him, all would have gone well. Unfortunately, he made a major decision based upon fear, which had consequences for both himself and the northern tribes.

Rehoboam obviously wanted control over all the tribes, and

he had one great asset that Jeroboam did not—the capital, Jerusalem, and more important, the temple of Solomon, which was the central feature in the religious lives of the people. Jeroboam began to ponder this perceived disadvantage, and the more he thought about it, the more his fears grew.

"And Jeroboam said in his heart, Now shall the kingdom return to the house of David: If this people go up to do sacrifice in the house of the Lord at Jerusalem, then shall the heart of this people turn again unto their lord, even unto Rehoboam king of Judah, and they shall kill me, and go again to Rehoboam king of Judah." (1 Kings 12:26–27.)

Jeroboam had convincing reasons to fear the revolt of the people. But the Lord had promised him through a prophet that he could have all that his soul desired and an established leadership over the people for generations. His fears were groundless as long as he followed the Lord. He then made a mistake we often make when the mist of fear begins to cloud our thinking. He sought for counsel, not from men of God but from men of the world.

"Whereupon the king took counsel, and made two calves of gold, and said unto them, It is too much for you to go up to Jerusalem: behold thy gods, O Israel, which brought thee up out of the land of Egypt. And he set the one in Beth-el, and the other put he in Dan." (1 Kings 12:28–29.) He also ordained new priests to serve his new gods and established a new national religious holiday to replace the Passover.

The result of these actions was foreseeable. The righteous priests of Jehovah fled to the kingdom of Judah, and with them went the righteous worshipers of Jehovah. "The Levites left their suburbs and their possession, and came to Judah and Jerusalem: for Jeroboam and his sons had cast them off from executing the priest's office unto the Lord. . . . And after them out of all the tribes of Israel such as set their hearts to seek the Lord God of Israel came to Jerusalem, to sacrifice unto the Lord

God of their fathers. So they strengthened the kingdom of Judah, and made Rehoboam the son of Solomon strong." (2 Chronicles 11:14–17.)

How ironic that the very thing Jeroboam most feared, the defection of his people to Rehoboam, became the costly consequence of his own fears. The northern kingdom never recovered from this drain of righteous people. From Jeroboam's decision of fear we can date the decline of the ten tribes that would lead to their "lost" state. We simply must not make decisions based on fear as did Jeroboam. When I am tempted to do so, I say to myself, "Have faith in the living God; don't mold your own golden calf."

Had Jeroboam believed the Lord's promises and made a decision of faith instead of fear, the whole history of the house of Israel would have been different. Instead, within one generation, the lineage of Jeroboam lost the leadership of Israel. His son Nadab ruled only two years before being overthrown by Baasha, who killed not only Nadab but "all the house of Jeroboam; he left not to Jeroboam any that breathed, until he had destroyed him." (1 Kings 15:29.)

DECISIONS OF FAITH

If we, ourselves, have not made decisions based on fear, we are probably aware of those who have. I am acquainted with a woman whose patriarchal blessing promised that if she remained faithful, she would marry a worthy husband in the temple and have a righteous posterity. With faith in this promise, she lived as best she could. However, as time passed and she finished college, she had not yet met her worthy husband. She began her employment and attended a singles ward, still anticipating that she would find her desired companion. But time continued to pass with no marriage prospects, and her fears mounted with every passing year. Finally she met a man at work who was not a member of the Church. He was kind to her, although he showed no interest in the Church. Fearing that she would never have another chance to get married, she accepted his proposal. In spite of her hopes that he would one day see the beauty of the gospel, his lack of interest continued, and their children are often torn between the standards of their parents. Unfortunately, stories like this one are far too common. The Lord had promised her a faithful, worthy companion, but the mist of fear set in, and she made a decision that, like Jeroboam's, had serious consequences for her children.

I suppose all bishops struggle, as they teach the blessings of tithing, to help members of their wards make decisions of faith instead of fear. Of all the commandments of the gospel, this one is most often thwarted by the mist of fear. Some people just can't see, logically, how less can be more in financial matters. But it is a matter of faith. We must believe that the Lord will truly "open . . . the windows of heaven, and pour [us] out a blessing, that there shall not be room enough to receive it. And . . . rebuke the devourer for [our] sakes." (Malachi 3:10–11.)

As I teach the college-age youth of the Church, I have seen their fear of making a mistake in marriage cripple their relationships. Of course, choosing an eternal companion is a critical decision and must be entered into with the deepest thought and prayer, but it is not as difficult as so many make it. Some people want an absolute revelation before entering into marriage. No one receives that promise. Eternal marriages are developed over long years of living the gospel, compromising and growing together, and forgiving and accepting one another's weaknesses. If we have made our decisions based on such important criteria as commitment to the gospel, personality and character traits, and the peaceful confirmation of the Spirit, we may go forward.

Sometimes when problems develop later in marriage, the adversary throws up the mist of fear in another manner, and the couple begins to fear that they made the wrong decision. This often paralyzes their ability to deal with problems and progress in becoming one. Surely they would be happier with someone else, they think. Often this type of reasoning leads to adultery, divorce, and sorrow. Perhaps some couples have made wrong decisions that cannot be corrected through mutual growth and a willingness to change. It may be that divorce is inevitable. But these cases will be rare if faith governs our thoughts rather than fear and doubt.

Young people often face decisions of fear that cause them to make tragic mistakes. Since friends are so important to them, they may do things they know are wrong out of fear that they will lose their friends. They may compromise their standards for fear of being mocked or laughed at. They may sacrifice virtue for fear of losing love. We must help them realize that no true friend would ever force a decision motivated by fear.

SHAKEN IN THE SPIRIT

When we allow fear to enter our thinking, we may block the power of the Lord to commune and counsel with us. Jacob was worried about this when his people were tempted with materialism, immorality, and racial prejudice. He loved his people and deeply desired to turn them back into the paths of righteousness. He told them, "I will unfold this mystery unto you; *if I do not, by any means, get shaken from my firmness in the Spirit, and stumble because of my over anxiety for you.*" (Jacob 4:18.)

It is especially important that parents recognize the mist of fear mentioned by Jacob. Parents have such love for their children. When one of them strays, anxiety and worry are natural. Parents need the guidance of the Spirit in such times, and anxiety and fear can shake them from the firmness of the Spirit. I believe that the expression "firmness in the Spirit" means we are confident that our decisions of what to do, what to say, and how to proceed are firm because we have received the guidance of the Spirit. Our fears and anxiety for the welfare of the child, however, may block that firmness, and we may be left wondering how to proceed.

We will all be tempted by the fears of Jeroboam from time to time during our lives. Let us have comfort in the love of the Lord for us. His promises are certain, and help is available for whatever we face. We must remember Mormon's words: "Perfect love casteth out all fear." (Moroni 8:16.) Love is a powerful spiritual quality. I believe that Mormon meant not only that our love for others has the ability to conquer our fears for them, but also that our understanding of God's love for us can overpower all our anxieties. Since we know we are the children of a loving Father, in time, if we have faith, all will be well.

CHAPTER FOURTEEN

FACING THE LION
AND THE BEAR

When I was growing up, baseball was the great American pastime. Like most young boys, I had a favorite team and a favorite player and was caught up in collecting baseball cards. For a nickel I could buy a package of five cards with the additional treat of a large wad of chewing gum to accompany them. My appetite for baseball cards grew so great that I could not earn enough nickels doing chores around the house for my mother to satisfy it.

Discovering that empty soda-pop bottles fetched three cents for a small one and a nickel for a large one, I began combing the fields and roadsides around our house for bottles. One day while foraging, I noticed the open garage door of a neighbor's house. Inside, lined up against the wall, was a veritable fortune in pop bottles. The temptation was too great, and I helped myself to the treasure trove. I soon discovered that many garages stored bottles.

I had a fort built in the rafters of the garage. There I stored my bottles, waiting to turn them all in, in one great baseball-card shopping spree. Before I could accomplish this, however, my mother came into the garage, noticed the glint of glass sparkling from the rafters, and asked me where I had gotten so many bottles. I confessed to my mother, who allowed me to determine what I should do. She knew it was important that I win this small victory on my own. "Bottles today," she thought, "something greater tomorrow."

I loaded my wagon with the bottles. I had one small problem: I could not remember where I had found them all, so I knocked on doors up and down the street asking the people if they had stored any bottles in their garage. To this day I remember the terrible feeling as I pulled my wagon up the street. It was not a feeling of embarrassment but something much deeper. Most people didn't care, and many told me to keep them. To them a pop bottle was an insignificant thing, but to a small boy a foundation of honesty was being laid.

HE "SHALL BE AS ONE OF THEM"

One of the mists all of us have to face early in our lives is the suggestion that small deviations from the strait and narrow path don't matter. However, those early memories provide a foundation for later challenges, and hence we greatly limit the tempter's power if we win them. We might call this facing the lion and the bear.

When the Israelites were challenged by the Philistine champion, Goliath, not a single one had the courage to face him, including Saul, who "from his shoulders and upward . . . was higher than any of the people." (1 Samuel 9:2.) When David entered the camp and heard Goliath's defiance of Israel's God, David said to Saul, "Let no man's heart fail because of him; thy servant will go and fight with this Philistine." (1 Samuel 17:32.)

Saul was not convinced. "Thou art not able to go against this Philistine to fight with him," he said, "for thou art but a youth, and he a man of war from his youth." (1 Samuel 17:33.) However, David had won earlier victories against lesser enemies, and those victories gave him the faith and the courage needed to face the present danger: "Thy servant kept his father's sheep, and there came a lion, and a bear, and took a lamb out of the flock: and I went out after him, and smote him. . . . Thy servant slew both the lion and the bear: and this uncircumcised Philistine shall be as one of them. . . . The Lord that delivered me out of the paw of the lion, and out of the paw of the bear, he will deliver me out of the hand of this Philistine." (1 Samuel 17:34–37.)

As I have taught the youth of the Church and conversed with their parents, I have noticed that two basic attitudes prevail. Some feel that the lion and bear choices are not that critical. If their children date a time or two before they are sixteen, where is the harm? Others believe these early decisions provide the strength needed later for future battles with greater Goliaths.

CRY FOR STRENGTH

The Nephites, aware of the growing strength of the Gadianton robbers, knew that one day they would have to face them. They were instructed to "cry unto the Lord *for strength* against the time that the robbers should come down against them." (3 Nephi 3:12.) What was true of their physical threat is also true of our spiritual ones. Eventually temptations and spiritual attacks will come. Before they arrive, we must cry for strength to meet them. That strength often comes through lion and bear experiences.

We will undoubtedly discover sooner or later that the Lord has a number of ways he can strengthen us for future difficulties. Life itself has a way of preparing us. Most of us will face lion and bear situations before we are asked to meet the Goliaths of our life. In light of this, it is critical that we defeat the lion and the bear first. From those experiences we gather strength. President Spencer W. Kimball taught, "One of the numerous rewards in girding ourselves to do hard things is in the creation of a capacity for doing of the still harder things." (*Teachings of Spencer W. Kimball,* ed. Edward L. Kimball [Salt Lake City: Bookcraft, 1982], p. 362.)

Other scripture stories affirm the truth of David's experience. As a Primary child I learned of the early decision of Daniel and his three friends, Hananiah, Mishael, and Azariah: "Daniel purposed in his heart that he would not defile himself with the portion of the king's meat, nor with the wine which he drank." (Daniel 1:8.) This is the first story we read in the book of Daniel. Some might have considered this refusal to violate the Mosaic Word of Wisdom a minor point. They were being honored and trained by the Babylonian king, so why risk offense? The rest of the book of Daniel, however, is the result of that early decision. It was the lion and bear moment in their lives.

"As for these four children, God gave them knowledge and skill in all learning and wisdom: and Daniel had understanding in all visions and dreams." (Daniel 1:17.) The link between the first chapter of Daniel and the rest of the book is obvious. The rest of the book of Daniel contains his many revelations, visions, and dreams. Does not our own Word of Wisdom promise that those who obey it "shall find wisdom and great treasures of knowledge, even hidden treasures"? (D&C 89:19.) Had he not won that first small victory, I do not believe any of us would have ever heard of him, just as we undoubtedly would not have heard of a young man named David if he had not fought a lion and bear and defeated them.

"A RARE ACT OF MORAL COURAGE"

When I was a junior in high school, I came under the influence of a brilliant English teacher. She was tough on her students, always insisting that they clearly and thoroughly defend any position they took. One day while discussing Dante's *Divine*

Comedy, she said that Christian religions teach that mankind are sent to two places after death, heaven and hell.

I raised my hand and said, "Not all Christians believe that." I thought that would be the end of it, but she replied, "Oh, which religion believes differently?" I was trapped now. I briefly answered with the Church's teachings about the three degrees of glory. She then turned to the class and said, "Class, is there anyone here who would like to ask Mr. Wilcox about his position?" I was terrified. The class was filled with the top students of the school. They were intelligent and confident and represented many different religions. I felt both scholastically and socially out of my league. I was the only Latter-day Saint and would have no help.

There followed a full discussion that took the entire class period while student after student challenged my beliefs. I remember feeling I had made a bad decision to raise my hand at the beginning of the class. The teacher did not say a word for most of the period; she just let the questions and arguments flow while she sat on her stool and watched.

I kept glancing at the clock and prayed for the bell. I felt that I was doing a poor job of defending my beliefs. Just minutes before the period ended, the teacher stopped the attacks and with her words turned that frightening experience into a lion and bear foundation for me. She said, "We have all had fun at the expense of Mr. Wilcox, but I would like to ask each of you if you could have defended your beliefs as he has. Today, we have all witnessed a rare act of moral courage, and I compliment Mr. Wilcox."

I could hardly believe what I was hearing. Coming from her, it was the highest compliment I had received. She taught me that day that I could, and should, stand for my values and beliefs. There have followed more delicate and pressured situations where challenges have been more severe and critical, but the memory of that day has strengthened me. I believe the Lord may have had a hand in that day's events. Perhaps, knowing how valuable this would be throughout my life, the Lord motivated a teacher to turn the lions and bears of her class loose on a young man. I am grateful for the strength she gave me.

VICTORIES OF PAST GENERATIONS

It is good to be able to say, "I have faced the lion and the bear, and I know I can now face Goliath." It is also important that we write these moments down, and that we share them with our children. Sometimes a lion and bear challenge in the life of a parent will prepare children for their own Goliaths. Numerous times I have been strengthened by the memory of how my mother or an ancestor faced a personal challenge.

Lucifer greatly desires that we lose the lion and bear battles. He is pleased when the victories of one generation are not recorded and eventually forgotten. He suggests to us constantly that these little victories or defeats don't really matter. Nephi revealed this mist of the tempter when he described the rationalization of people in the last days: "Eat, drink, and be merry; nevertheless, fear God—he will justify in committing a little sin; yea, lie a little, take the advantage of one because of his words, dig a pit for thy neighbor; there is no harm in this." (2 Nephi 28:8.) In a sense, however, these last words may be true. God is deeply merciful, and we are all going to commit "little" sins. "Where is the harm in these?" we may ask. But as my mother knew as she stared at the bottles in the rafters of the garage, "Bottles today, something greater tomorrow." In like manner may we all remember that defeating lions and bears today leads to defeating Goliaths tomorrow.

CHAPTER FIFTEEN

THE MEANEST COW IN THE WORLD

When I was young I sometimes had to milk the cows. We had a big, black milk cow we named Meanie. She was the meanest cow in the world. She hated being milked and hated everyone who made the attempt. I think she took it as a personal affront that anyone would take her milk to feed lowly humans instead of obviously superior calves.

She used to charge us whenever we tried to get her into the corral for milking. Often she would hide in the willows and wait for us to walk by, then bolt out and try to pin us to the ground. Milking her was a horrendous affair. Few people could accomplish it. My uncle would rope her, then loop the rope around a fence pole and pull her up next to it. This usually required choking her half to death before she would quit fighting. He then tied her head snug against the fence, wrapped the rope around her body, and tied her tail to the fence. Then he looped the rope around her outside back leg and pulled it off the ground, tying it to the fence so she couldn't kick with it. After this, she grudgingly consented to be milked. Even then, if he didn't tie the ropes good and tight, she would free her hind leg and kick over the milk bucket.

I really hated that cow. She scared me half to death, and I hated going after her in the evenings, for she was especially mean just before sunset. I used to wonder why my uncle put up with her. I would have sold her for sausages long ago. She did have one redeeming feature: she gave sweeter milk, and more of it, than any other cow on the ranch.

One day when she had been especially mean and even my uncle was having difficulty controlling his temper, I asked him, "Why is Meanie so mean?"

"Because she thinks she's a wild range cow," he answered, "and range cows like to run free."

"Why don't you let her be a range cow?" I countered. "Why don't you just leave her alone and get another one? There are lots of milk cows."

"Because she's not a range cow," he responded. "She's a milk cow, and a darn good one. She just doesn't know it yet. We're trying to teach her."

I don't recall if any of us ever succeeded in teaching Meanie to behave, but the memory of her and my conversation with my uncle has stayed with me. Occasionally we meet people, especially youth, who seem to fight all efforts to work with them. They kick against the ropes. Sometimes it is tempting just to let them run wild. But the Lord never gives up on them, and I can imagine Him saying to us, "They think they are children of the world, but we know better. They are my children. They just don't know it yet. We're trying to teach them."

CHILDREN OF GOD

I believe that the one doctrine Lucifer fears the most, and wants most to keep deeply veiled in his mists, is the conviction that we are literal sons and daughters of God. Inherent in that knowledge is the realization that we can one day be like Him.

Satan has tempted some of the greatest people in the scriptural record to doubt this powerful truth. There is nothing that clears the mists of the world more effectively than a sharp understanding of who we really are.

During a conversation with Moses, God addressed him three times as "my son." One of those three times He added the following description: "Thou art in the similitude of mine Only Begotten; and mine Only Begotten is and shall be the Savior, for he is full of grace and truth." (Moses 1:4, 6, 7.) God then showed Moses the world and all its inhabitants. After this vision Moses "was left to himself," and Satan came tempting him, saying, "Moses, son of man, worship me." (Moses 1:12.) There are two temptations in the devil's words. The obvious, outward one is to worship him; the more subtle, suggested one is found in the words *son of man.* "You're not a son of God," Lucifer is saying. "You're just a man."

Moses did not give in to either temptation and responded with a mist-clearing statement that all people need to believe: "Who art thou? *For behold, I am a son of God, in the similitude of his Only Begotten;* and where is thy glory, that I should worship thee?" (Moses 1:13.)

Secure in the knowledge of who he was and in whose similitude he desired to remain, Moses cleared the mist of doubt cast upon him by Lucifer. Satan tried this same mist upon the Savior himself. After being baptized, Jesus heard the Father say to Him, "Thou art my beloved son; in thee I am well pleased." (Luke 3:22.) He immediately went into the wilderness to fast and pray in preparation for His coming ministry. After His fasting, Satan tempted Him three times. As he did with Moses, he combined a subtle temptation with a direct one: "If thou be the Son of God, command that these stones be made bread." (Matthew 4:3.) Stones to bread is the direct temptation, but the more powerful one is contained in the word *if.* We find this word again in the second temptation: "If thou be the Son of

God, cast thyself down." (Matthew 4:6.) Even in the last moments of His agony while on the cross, the challenge to His divine Sonship was thrown at His feet: "If thou be the Son of God, come down from the cross." (Matthew 27:40.) Nothing else so maddened Jesus' opponents as His assertion that He was God's Son. And no other doctrine of the Restoration so distresses our detractors as the belief in our divine parentage and what that means for our future destiny.

Christ gave in to none of these suggestions. He knew who He was, just as did Moses. We, too, must know who we are. There is a reason why Lucifer is so anxious to cloud the vision of our true identity. John, in his first epistle, explains that reason and why it is so important that we see through this mist:

"Behold, what manner of love the Father hath bestowed upon us, that we should be called the sons of God: therefore the world knoweth us not, because it knew him not. Beloved, now are we the sons of God, and it doth not yet appear what we shall be: but we know that, when he shall appear, we shall be like him; for we shall see him as he is. *And every man that hath this hope in him purifieth himself, even as he is pure.*" (1 John 3:1–3.) If we truly believe that we are the children of God, we will live up to our heritage.

CARRION WITH THE BUZZARDS

I was once driving on a dirt road far from any town, when I rounded a corner and saw a large flock of buzzards feasting on some carrion in the middle of the road. Buzzards are ugly. They have no feathers on their heads, and their skin is red. Their feathers are dusty brown. They have their purpose, but not many really admire them. There must have been about fifteen of them squabbling and fighting over the dead animal in the road.

One of them, however, looked much larger than the others. I had never before seen a buzzard that big. He towered above the others. As my truck drew near, the buzzards began to fly off—all but the large one in the center. He seemed hesitant to leave the carrion and stayed long after the others had scattered. I had to slow down to avoid hitting him. When I was very close, I could see that he was not a buzzard at all but a golden eagle.

I love to see the eagles circle and ride the air currents of the canyons. This was the first time I had seen such a magnificent bird accompanied by buzzards feasting on road kill. I felt a stab of sorrow that such a beautiful bird had stooped to sharing such an unwholesome meal with such unwelcoming fellows.

PASTURES IN HIGH PLACES

Babylon is described by John as "a cage of every unclean and hateful bird." (Revelation 18:2.) We are the chosen and elect children of our eternal Father in Heaven. We are eagles, meant to circle high above the things of Babylon in the freedom of the heavens. We were not meant to sit in the dust of the road feasting on the carrion of the world with the buzzards. Much of the world feeds on carrion not fit for a child of God. We see it in the movies and on television. We hear it in music and read it in magazines and books. We sense it in the styles and fashions of the day and see it in the lifestyles of celebrities.

We must rise above it all, secure in our knowledge of who we are, motivated by the assurance of what we can be in our Father's eternal worlds. In the book of Isaiah the Lord encourages us to flee Babylon and touch not their unclean things. (See Isaiah 52:11.) He promises all who are willing to depart that "their pastures shall be in all high places." (Isaiah 49:9.)

Lucifer hopes that if he can get us to see ourselves as belonging with the buzzards, to acquire a taste for the carrion of Babylon, we will forget our true identity and lose our taste for eternal things. That is why we must teach our children to believe the words they sing in Primary, "I am a child of God," and must bring them up "in light and truth" as instructed by the

Lord. (D&C 93:40.) Then, and only then, will the darkest mist of that fallen angel be dispersed.

"I CAN JUDGE"

There is a critical need to avoid feasting on the carrion of the world and to teach children early in their lives how to do so. One of the most effective ways of accomplishing this is taught to us by Moses during his encounter with Satan. "Blessed be the name of my God," Moses said, "for his Spirit hath not altogether withdrawn from me, or else where is thy glory, for it is darkness unto me? And I *can judge between thee and God. . . .* I will not cease to call upon God, I have other things to inquire of him: *for his glory has been upon me, wherefore I can judge between him and thee. Depart hence, Satan.*" (Moses 1:15, 18.)

Moses knew to reject darkness because he had first seen light and knew the difference. So it is with good and evil. Understanding this, there are two approaches we may take to guide us through life. One is obviously better than the other. We are here to learn the difference between good and evil. How shall we accomplish this? Some say, "By experiencing darkness I will know what light is." The others say, "Let us first experience light and then we will know to shun the darkness."

Speaking in practical terms, if I want my children to read only things that are edifying, I must read to them such works when they are small, so that later when the world presents them with literature that is not virtuous, they will know the difference. If I want them to watch only the best, most praiseworthy movies, I must raise them on these while they are young. This is true of music, clothing, and everything else.

We must realize that a taste for the evil, unclean things of the world will in time destroy the taste for the wholesome, good things of life—just as a taste for what is "virtuous, lovely, or of good report, or praiseworthy" will overpower the taste for the

crude, the vulgar, the suggestive, and the carnal. (Articles of
Faith 1:13.) Lucifer knows this, and one of his mists is to convince parents not to strongly instill in their children the teachings of the gospel while they are young. Instead, they say, they
will allow them to choose for themselves later in life. They will
not "force" their children to accept their beliefs or standards.

Although this sounds good on the surface, in reality it is a
mist thrown up in the hope that the taste for the good things
God's children so naturally crave in childhood may be replaced
by a taste for the things of the world. By the time these children
are ready to make their own choices, the choices have already
been made. Learning to love the light can be acquired later in
life, but it is more difficult than growing up in the light and
loving it from the start.

"THEY DIDN'T KILL THE WOLF, DID THEY?"

The propensity of God's children to gravitate toward the
light was shown to me one evening when I decided to show my
children a movie. They were all under eight years old at the
time. I brought home Disney's *Davy Crockett*. All went well
until the frontiersmen began to shoot the Indians. My children
were much distressed by this, and my son asked, "They didn't
kill them, did they?" When I heard this question, I realized that
my children had the proper attitude toward war and fighting.

The next night I decided to play it safe and brought home a
cartoon—*Peter and the Wolf*. All went well until they brought
home the wolf swinging on a pole between two hunters. Once
again there was distress in the Wilcox household. "They didn't
kill the wolf, did they?" my daughter asked. I had to respond,
"No, they are just taking him to the zoo so he can't eat any
more of Peter's little forest friends."

I am not suggesting that we stop watching *Davy Crockett* or
Peter and the Wolf. I use these examples only to point out the
deep, innate goodness of the Lord's children. That goodness is

a great ally. In time, life in this world will take its toll upon this godly sensitivity, but the more we can surround ourselves and our children with the best things in life, the more able we and they will be to see through the mists of Satan. Even in the darkest temptations, when purity and beauty are difficult to perceive, the memory of all God's bright, burning light will strengthen us, and we will instinctively turn away from the baser choices of the world.

CHAPTER SIXTEEN

THE GREAT MAGICIAN

While on his mission, one of my sons learned a few magic tricks to entertain children he met in church or on the street. This developed into a full-blown interest when he returned home. Now he can really astound the family with a large array of disappearances, changes, and so on. One day while teaching a class of teenagers, after amazing them with a trick or two, he asked, "Who is the greatest magician, and what is the greatest trick?" The class supplied a number of answers, naming past and present magicians, before my son directed them to two scriptures as hints: "And no marvel," Paul wrote to the Corinthians, "for Satan himself is transformed into an angel of light. Therefore it is no great thing if his ministers also be transformed as the ministers of righteousness." (2 Corinthians 11:14–15.) The greatest magician is Satan. His greatest trick is plainly stated by Isaiah, who warns all generations to be careful lest we "call evil good, and good evil; . . . put darkness for light, and light for darkness; . . . put bitter for sweet and sweet for bitter!" (Isaiah 5:20.) The greatest deception is the ability to make wrong appear right and good appear evil.

EXAGGERATED VIRTUES

One of the most effective and common ways the tempter reverses values is to make one virtue seem all-inclusive. Any virtue pushed to the extreme will begin to destroy all others. For example, in a previous chapter we discussed using freedom to justify rebellion. President Boyd K. Packer taught, "Interesting how one virtue, when given exaggerated or fanatical emphasis, can be used to batter down another, with freedom, a virtue, invoked to protect *vice*." (*Ensign*, May 1992, p. 66.) Those who justify sin in the name of freedom view themselves as defending the good. "How can anyone who opposes freedom possibly be taken seriously?" they argue. Those who challenge their position are labeled evil—ostensibly because they are against freedom, liberty, or choice.

There are two other areas besides freedom where this mist has widespread effectiveness in turning good to evil and evil to good—tolerance and love. Both of these virtues are extremely important in our interpersonal relations, but they have been used to countenance some of the most serious infractions of eternal law.

I was interested in the reaction of many funding organizations, community leaders, and businesses to the stand taken by the Boy Scouts of America to maintain the Scout Oath, which ends with the words "morally straight." Court cases were filed attempting to force the Scouts to accept homosexual Scoutmasters. The Scouting movement won its case in the United States Supreme Court by a slim 5-to-4 margin. Funds were cut off, access to public schools threatened, and business support dropped. Each of these institutions, and the individuals who made the decisions, were motivated, in their own minds, by a desire to be tolerant of an alternative lifestyle. Rather than seeing the Scouts as trying to maintain a level of morality, they viewed them as intolerant and puritanical. One of the finest organizations in America for developing young men was now not worthy of support, in their estimation. Good had turned to evil, light to darkness, and sweet to bitter.

The scriptures shed light on the modern chorus that demands tolerance of all choices. In the book of Acts, Philip was directed to talk with an Ethiopian who was puzzled about a prophecy from Isaiah. After Philip explained that the prophecy described the mission of the Savior, the Ethiopian desired baptism. "See, here is water," he said. "*What doth hinder me to be baptized?*" (Acts 8:36.) He was anxious to do what was necessary, to make the alterations in his life that he needed to be a disciple of Jesus. Was there anything else that stopped him? The modern, mist-blinded world says, "Accept me the way I am, without asking me to change." The true disciple asks, "What changes must I make to be acceptable to the Lord?" Lamoni's father demonstrated this attitude when he prayed, "I will give away all my sins to know thee." (Alma 22:18.)

Although the rich young ruler did not have the courage to follow the Savior's counsel, he exhibited the same sentiment when he asked, "What lack I yet?" (Matthew 19:20.) Though he had kept the commandments from his youth, he was still ready to make adjustments. The sincerity of the young man is evident in the Savior's response: "Then Jesus beholding him *loved him.*" (Mark 10:21.) This willingness to change is obviously pleasing to the Lord. However, the world sees this attitude as giving in to intolerance. The Savior shows us the right balance of tolerance and love for the sinner while remaining unequivocally opposed to sin. There is never any doubt how He felt about the people He taught, regardless of how they were living, but there is also no doubt that He could not look upon sin with any degree of allowance, and that He expected them to leave their destructive habits.

"BRIDLE ALL YOUR PASSIONS"

The great magician's trick of making evil appear good is also evident when the world speaks of love. A young couple sat in my office one Sunday desiring a temple recommend in order to be married. I was unable to give them one as soon as they desired because of some moral transgressions. They were somewhat shocked that they could not go immediately to the temple. "We bent the rules," they said, "but we love each other." Somehow, in their minds, love justified physical intimacy before marriage. But the truth is, if they loved each other enough, that love would have restrained them. I have heard people justify even adultery and the breakup of families by saying, "We love each other." That which they call love is in reality a mist, one sometimes difficult to distinguish, but a mist all the same. This mist shrouds love in the darkness of selfishness and incontinence.

Paul urged the Saints, "Walk in love, as Christ also hath loved us. . . . But fornication, and all uncleanness, or covetousness, let it not be once named among you, as becometh saints." (Ephesians 5:2–3.) Paul was suggesting that if the Saints really loved each other, fornication and other uncleanness would disappear. Love is the motivation for staying worthy for the temple, not fuel for giving in to physical demands.

Alma the Younger counseled his son Shiblon in like manner: "See that ye *bridle* all your passions, that ye *may be filled with love*." (Alma 38:12.) Love can be a bridle that controls passion. Alma assures us that controlling passion increases love. The world reverses this truth, asserting that releasing passion is an act of love. That the world is deceived by this mist is not surprising; that the Saints sometimes are is cause for sorrow.

SEARCH IN THE LIGHT OF CHRIST

Moroni knew that in the latter days people would call good evil and evil good. He therefore included in the last pages of the Book of Mormon counsel his father, Mormon, gave to the Saints who lived in the last days of the Nephite civilization. They too had difficulty clearing this mist, so Mormon gave them a key:

"Every thing which *inviteth* and *enticeth to do good,* and to *love God,* and to *serve him,* is inspired of God. Wherefore, take heed, my beloved brethren, that ye do not judge that which is evil to be of God, or that which is good and of God to be of the devil. For behold, my brethren, it is given unto you to judge, that ye may know good from evil; and the way to judge is as plain, that ye may know with a perfect knowledge, as the daylight is from the dark night. For behold, the *Spirit of Christ* is given to every man, that he may know good from evil; wherefore I show unto you the way to judge; for every thing which *inviteth to do good,* and to *persuade to believe in Christ,* is sent forth by the power and gift of Christ; wherefore ye may know with a perfect knowledge it is of God. . . . And now, my brethren, seeing that ye know the light by which ye may judge, which light is the light of Christ, see that ye do not judge wrongfully. . . . Wherefore, I beseech of you, brethren, that ye should *search diligently in the light of Christ* that ye may know good from evil; and if ye will *lay hold upon every good thing,* and condemn it not, ye certainly will be a child of Christ." (Moroni 7:13–19.)

Notice all the key words and phrases Mormon gives us to clear this mist of reversed values. We all have the light of Christ, an inner guide, which, if we are honest with ourselves, will direct us through this mist. We also have the life of the Savior as a model. If we study that life and become immersed in the spirit of the Master, we will know instinctively what is good and what is evil. We can ask ourselves these types of questions suggested by Mormon: Will this action increase my love of God? Does it create in me a desire to serve Him more? Would the Savior do the same thing if He were in my position? Does it strengthen my faith in the Savior? Would Christ call my actions good? Do I sense a spirit of invitation and persuasion to do good, or am I being enticed to gratify my personal desires or passions? Would I feel comfortable in telling the Savior about my decision and what I have done? Do I desire to "lay hold" on this action, or, in other words, to keep doing it again and again?

Mormon also encourages us to "search diligently" in the light of Christ. This suggests that effort is required on our part. We must not passively wait for good to come around; instead, we must actively look for it. The search itself becomes a defense against mistaking evil for good or good for evil. Does not the thirteenth article of faith also encourage us to actively "seek after" that which is "virtuous, lovely, or of good report, or praiseworthy"?

A COLLECTION OF GOOD THINGS

Mormon told his people to lay hold upon every good thing. Later in this same speech he told them to "cleave unto every good thing." (Moroni 7:28.) When I was younger, I collected coins. The man who owned the coin shop had collected so long that he could spot a counterfeit at a glance. This is true of almost anything people choose to collect. The more they surround themselves with the genuine article, the easier they can detect false copies. So it is in spiritual matters. The more good we lay hold on and cleave to, the easier it will be to discern the counterfeits. Some decisions, thoughts, feelings, and actions will simply not fit with the rest of our collected good deeds. While we are young and have not yet accumulated a large enough collection to discern easily, we must trust the master collectors, those who have done good throughout a lifetime. Let the prophets and the great men and women in the scriptures train us until our own collection of righteousness is accumulated and our ability to discern refined. Then, as Mormon said, we "may know with a perfect knowledge, as the daylight is from the dark night" how to distinguish the bitter from the sweet, the good from the evil.

On a few occasions my son has shown me how he accomplishes his feats of magic. I always feel a letdown. The deception is so simple, the explanation so unspectacular, that I feel somewhat of a fool for not having seen through it. I wonder if at the great day of judgment, when all the tricks and deceptions of the great magician, the adversary, are made known, those who have been deceived will feel a similar pain, but augmented a hundredfold because the consequences are so much more serious. No one need feel that letdown. The mist can be cleared in this life, if we will only make use of the truths the Lord so freely grants us.

CHAPTER SEVENTEEN

CROWNING A KING

My family enjoys visiting the national parks of America. We have hiked in many of them and love to feel the sense of childlike wonder the creations of the Lord inspire. In most of these parks, wildlife abounds, and because the animals have become accustomed to human visitors, they are often quite tame. At the scenic turnouts, in the campgrounds, and even in the backcountry, wild animals approach visitors for a handout. The temptation to feed them is great, even though signs everywhere warn of the danger, which is most acute for the animals themselves. If fed too much, they develop a dependency on human handouts and often starve later because they have lost the ability to search for, or consume, their natural foods. So we constantly remind ourselves, *"Don't feed the squirrels."*

Can Lucifer take positive feelings, even feelings of love, compassion, and mercy, and turn them into a mist? I believe he can and does. Even the wisest and most noble may find their judgment obscured by such mists. Joseph Smith taught, "There must be decision of character, aside from sympathy." (*Teachings of the Prophet Joseph Smith,* selected by Joseph Fielding Smith

[Salt Lake City: Deseret Book Co., 1976], p. 202.) This is good counsel, for misguided sympathy and kindness may become, if not tempered with experience, judgment, and wisdom, a mist. I call these misguided decisions "crowning a king."

SUFFER THEM TO HAVE A KING

An excellent example of "feeding the squirrels" is found in the book of Ether. Few people in the scriptures are greater than the brother of Jared, whose name was Mahonri Moriancumr. His humility, his faith, and his close relationship with the Lord are well known. Through his instrumentality his people crossed the ocean with light in their barges and obtained the promised land. We know little of his or Jared's life after they arrived in America, but we are shown their last fateful decision.

As Jared and his brother grew old and sensed that they would soon die, his brother said to Jared, "Let us gather together our people that we may number them, that we may know of them what they will desire of us before we go down to our graves." (Ether 6:19.) Perhaps he thought the people would like a final blessing or instruction such as that given by Adam when he gathered his people just before his death. At any rate, the people were gathered and numbered. The brothers then asked for their final request. But they were not prepared for the answer: "The people desired of them that they should anoint one of their sons to be a king over them. And now behold, *this was grievous unto them.* And the brother of Jared said unto them: Surely this thing leadeth into captivity." (Ether 6:22–23.)

What do parents do when their children ask for something that is not right? How can mature wisdom direct foolish desires? And how can they direct without prompting their children to rebel? Every parent has faced such situations. Because most parents want their children to like them as well as love them, because facing their protestations is often painful and difficult, there is a tendency to give in. Parents may opt for the immediate gratification of their approval rather than focus on their long-term happiness. Jared and his brother were apparently no different. They feared that their people's request would in time lead to disaster, but the people were insistent, for they asked the brother of Jared to force his son to fill the position.

The result? His foresight was set aside. "Suffer them that they may have a king," Jared said—a decision of sympathy rather than character. (Ether 6:24.)

Knowing how their fathers felt about the request, all the sons of the brother of Jared and all but one son of Jared refused to be king. Finally Orihah accepted the post. At first everything went smoothly. Orihah was a good and righteous king. Perhaps, during his reign and even during the reign of his son, Kib, the people would have said, "What was all the worry about? Look how great things are going. Why were our parents so concerned about a king?"

However, in the reign of Kib, disaster began to strike as son fought father and brother fought brother for control of the kingdom, leading to civil war and corruption. The Book of Ether was written to warn us about being blinded by the mists of misguided kindness—to teach us that sometimes we must simply say no, even at the risk of disappointment and anger.

CHECKING A CHILD

President Joseph F. Smith counseled the Saints about "king-crowning" decisions: "God forbid that there should be any of us so unwisely indulgent, so thoughtless and so shallow in our affection for our children that we dare not check them in a wayward course, in wrong-doing and in their foolish love for the things of the world more than for the things of righteousness, for fear of offending them. I want to say this: Some people have grown to possess such unlimited confidence in their children that they do not believe it possible for them to be led astray or do wrong. . . . The result is, they turn them loose, morning, noon, and night, to attend all kinds of entertainments and amusements, often in company with those whom they know not and do not understand." (*Gospel Doctrine*, 5th ed. [Salt Lake City: Deseret Book Co., 1939], p. 286.)

"THE VASSALAGE OF THEIR OWN DELUSIONS"

These principles are also applicable in leadership positions, both civic and religious. When Moses was on Mt. Sinai, the people demanded of Aaron that he make them a golden calf. He gave in, turning the people over to their lower passions and beliefs. When Moses challenged him, saying, "What did this people unto thee, that thou hast brought so great a sin upon them?" Aaron responded, "Thou knowest the people, that they are set on mischief." (Exodus 32:21–22.) It is sometimes difficult for a leader to say no to the people when they are "set on" having their way. Many a bishop has faced youth leaders or parents who want activities outside the financial or distance guidelines of the handbooks. How can he direct their desires within the counsels of the Lord without offending them?

It takes a certain type of courage to dispel these mists. I am deeply impressed by a statement made by President John Quincy Adams when he had to make an unpopular political decision in his home state of Massachusetts. He supported a policy of the opposing party against the wishes of his constituents and, in effect, committed political suicide. When asked about his decision, he said, "Highly as I reverenced the authority of my constituents, and bitter as would have been the cup of resistance to their declared will . . . I would have defended their interests against their inclinations, and incurred every possible addition to their resentment, to save them from the vassalage of their own delusions." (John F. Kennedy, *Profiles in Courage* [Harper and Row: New York, 1955].)

FOLLOWING THE LORD'S PATTERN

Perhaps we can learn from the Lord how to handle situations where the mists of sympathy, love, and kindness threaten to cloud experience and wisdom. He, too, is a father and is constantly confronted by the unwise desires of His children. When the Israelites gave in to the herd-instinct mist, asking Samuel for a king so they could be "like all the nations" (1 Samuel 8:5), the Lord was faced with a "king-crowning" moment. How did he deal with it?

The Lord counseled Samuel, "Hearken unto their voice: howbeit yet protest solemnly unto them, and shew them the manner of the king that shall reign over them." (1 Samuel 8:9.) In this verse the Lord revealed three things we might contemplate when faced with our own "king-crowning" moments:

1. He respected their agency. Even though He knew the final outcome of their desires, He granted them the freedom to choose.

2. He nevertheless protested "solemnly" against their desire. He made sure they understood clearly how much He was opposed to their declared intentions.

3. He carefully explained what the consequences of their decision would be. Samuel told them exactly what the king would eventually be like when corrupted by the power of the office.

The Lord also did a fourth thing that we read about several chapters later. "Fear not," Samuel told the people. "Ye have done all this wickedness: yet turn not aside from following the Lord, but serve the Lord with all your heart; and turn ye not aside: for then should ye go after vain things, which cannot profit nor deliver; for they are vain. *For the Lord will not forsake his people.* . . . Moreover as for me, God forbid that I should sin against the Lord in ceasing to pray for you: but I will teach you the good and the right way." (1 Samuel 12:20–23.)

The Lord was not vindictive; He chose the best person He could to be their king. He then gave them a new set of guidelines that, if followed, might still save them in spite of their foolishness. They could not live the highest law, so rather than completely abandon them to their own devices, He gave them a lower law they might be able to live. This is the same way He handled the children of Israel when they rebelled against Him in the wilderness.

God would not forsake His people; neither must we forsake our children or those we lead when they insist that we "crown for them a king." Like Samuel, we must continue to pray for them and teach them the good way. When an absolute "no" will not satisfy the people's will—when the king must be crowned in spite of all protests—the Lord's four-step plan may still save them. In time, they may learn to trust mature wisdom instead of foolish desire. While they are learning, parents or leaders must be careful not to say too often, "Suffer them that they may have a king."

CHAPTER EIGHTEEN

DON'T LICK GRASS

The chore I most hated as a boy was fixing fence. It was a hot, miserable job, and it was extremely boring. Hour after hour we would walk the miles of barbed-wire fence lines. We would stop where the cattle had stretched the wires or broken the posts and repair the damage. I knew how most of the holes and broken posts had been made.

It didn't much matter where you put the fence; the cows always felt there was better grass on the other side. I'm convinced that the expression "The grass is always greener on the other side" was invented by a cow. The middle of the meadow could be full of good, green grass, but the cows would wander the fence line looking greedily through the wires. Then they would stick their heads through the wire and eat the grass on the other side. Slowly the wires would stretch.

Not satisfied with this, they would eventually push against the wire, stretching their long tongues out as far as they could, and lick the grass into their mouths. In time the fence would break down, the posts would weaken, and huge holes would appear up and down the line.

The Lord has built some fairly sturdy fences to protect His

children. There is plenty of good, green grass in the middle of His meadow, but far too often we look longingly through His fence to the entertainments, pleasures, ambitions, fashions, and desires of the world. Many Church members would never think of actually breaking out of the Lord's protecting fence, but they see no harm in poking their heads through the wires to reach outside as far as possible. Morally speaking, they are "licking grass." Occasionally some even want the Lord or His prophets to move the fence for their convenience.

IN THE CENTER OF OUR LANDS

Just before the coming of Christ in the Book of Mormon, the Nephites and the converted Lamanites faced a serious threat to their existence. The Gadianton robbers had become so powerful that the believers were forced to gather together for mutual protection. They stored enough food to last seven years, in which time they hoped to prevail over their enemies.

Feeling their own strength, they made a suggestion to their prophet-leader, Gidgiddoni. "Pray unto the Lord, and let us go up upon the mountains and into the wilderness, that we may fall upon the robbers and destroy them in their own lands."

Gidgiddoni, however, knew the folly of this line of thinking. "The Lord forbid," he warned them, "for if we should go up against them the Lord would deliver us into their hands; therefore *we will prepare ourselves in the center of our lands,* . . . and we will not go against them . . . ; therefore as the Lord liveth, if we do this he will deliver them into our hands." (3 Nephi 3:20–21.)

Gidgiddoni's wisdom as it applied to a temporal battle is also true of spiritual ones. We are much more likely to be victorious in temptation and trial if we stay "in the center" of the standards and commandments of the gospel. In the center, the Lord has provided more than enough good, nourishing things for a lifetime. The closer we stray to the dividing line, the more likely we are to be defeated.

Youth are particularly prone to "grass licking," especially when it relates to the standards in *For the Strength of Youth*. The youth are counseled not to date until age sixteen. But they may arrange to meet someone at the school dance, dance every dance with that person, and then ride home with him or her. This is grass-licking early dating.

Similarly, there are certain standards for movies. *For the Strength of Youth* notes that we should avoid entertainment that is "vulgar, immoral, inappropriate, suggestive, or pornographic in any way." Obviously these criteria will eliminate most of Hollywood's offerings. But would it not be all right, we may reason, to rent the movie, even if the rating is unacceptable, and then fast-forward through the compromising parts? This is grass-licking movie watching.

One of the most dangerous examples of grass licking comes when young people stray too close to the line physically in moral areas. Other examples are easy to find.

Adults, too, often have grass-licking temptations. One of the most common is a casual attitude toward wearing the temple garment. Adults must also be careful not to move too close to the fence line in their own choices of entertainment. Perhaps it is most important that the parents stay in the center, for an obvious reason.

THE ESCAPE OF THE CALVES

I noticed while taking care of cattle as a boy that more often than not the cows did not go through the holes they had created in the fence, but the calves did. Sometimes we would ride up the fence line and find a calf separated from its mother. Often it would be half starved and bawling to get back inside the fence next to the mother. The calves seemed to know how to escape through the holes the older cattle had made, but rarely did they know how to step back through those holes. If they were not found, sometimes they died.

This is the true tragedy of grass-licking obedience to the standards and counsels of the Church. Parents must be careful in their own pushing of the limits not to create holes that their children will slip through. Compromising, for example, on the types of movies we watch may create a hole that our children will crawl through to their own destruction. One generation's exception becomes the next generation's rule, as standards of behavior deteriorate. If the cows had stayed in the center of the meadow, no calf would have ever been lost.

SPIRITUAL EROSION

This truth is demonstrated in the introductory chapters to the book of Judges. The Lord gave clear instructions to the Israelites that they were to "drive out" the Canaanites from the land when they went in to possess it. Joshua worked diligently to accomplish this, but at his death there was still more work to do. In the first chapter of Judges we read over and over that the individual tribes "dwelt among the Canaanites, the inhabitants of the land: for they did not drive them out." (Judges 1:32; see 1:21–33.)

"Ye have not obeyed my voice," the Lord told them. "Why have ye done this?" (Judges 2:2.) The Lord knew that if the older generation did not control the environment their children would be raised in, the Canaanite gods would "be a snare" unto them. (Judges 2:3.) The older generation were not compromised by the values or the gods of the land, for they had been made strong in testimony by their experiences in the wilderness. But "there arose another generation after them, which knew not the Lord, nor yet the works which he had done for Israel. . . . And they forsook the Lord God of their fathers . . . and followed other gods, of the gods of the people that were round about them." (Judges 2:10–12.)

We can't help but see why the Lord put this story into the scriptures. It is a warning to every older generation to be cautious about what they tolerate in their homes and society. Elder Neal A. Maxwell strongly taught this truth in general conference: "All are free to choose, of course, and we would not have it otherwise. Unfortunately, however, when some choose slackness, they are choosing not only for themselves, but for the next generation and the next. Small equivocations in parents can produce large deviations in their children! Earlier generations in a family may have reflected dedication, while some in the current generation evidence equivocation. Sadly, in the next, some may choose dissension as erosion takes its toll." (Conference Report, October 1992, p. 89.)

We see this same erosion throughout the book of Judges. We are told that each new generation "corrupted themselves *more* than their fathers . . . ; they ceased not from their own doings, nor from their stubborn way." (Judges 2:19.) The majority of responsibility still remains with the individual child, but surely the earlier generation's grass-licking tolerance shares in the spiritual erosion.

MISSIONARY OPEN HOUSES?

I was recently struck by a comment made by my fourteen-year-old son as his older brother prepared for his mission. Parents have been counseled by Church leaders not to hold open houses for departing missionaries. However, tremendous pressure is put on parents to hold such open houses. It is a social, cultural pressure that simply assumes such gatherings will be held because they have been in the past. Such events, however, often disrupt Sunday services, put financial burdens on the missionary's family, or create a fanfare atmosphere for a missionary entering the field.

Like all parents, my wife and I felt this pressure and talked about what we would do. We were sorely tempted to disregard the counsel and hold the open house. It isn't a serious violation of Church counsel, we reasoned. But we finally opted for a family dinner after the block meetings were over.

A few days later we learned of an elder who had compromised the rules of his mission. It was not a flagrant violation but a foolish disregarding of mission rules that damaged the elder and the work. It was this setting that caused my youngest son to say, almost in passing and somewhat humorously, "His parents probably held an open house for him."

Since life turns sometimes on the tiniest of hinges, let us as parents, leaders, and teachers do our best to stay in the center of the meadow, avoiding the compromises that often lie at the fence line. These decisions may in time be critical for our children and grandchildren, and for those we teach and influence in our callings.

CHAPTER NINETEEN

STANDING ON
THE PINNACLE

The Lord told the Prophet Joseph Smith, "The devil . . . rebelled against me . . . ; and also a third part of the hosts of heaven *turned he away from me* because of their agency." (D&C 29:36.) How is it possible that the tempter can turn God's children away from Him when our Father is so loving and compassionate? Remember, one of the specific reasons for the mists in Lehi's dream was to obscure the tree of life, which represented God's love. Most often Satan uses that loving and compassionate character to raise questions in our minds and cause us to doubt our inclusion in God's care. In the war in heaven, the suggestion was made that the Father's plan would not save all, whereas Lucifer's changes to that plan would include all of the Father's children. Who, therefore, loved them most? Those spirits who accepted that line of reasoning might question their Father's love and turn away.

In an earthly context, we might ask, "Since God is so filled with love, why does He not demonstrate that love by fulfilling our needs and desires? Why does He allow such negative things to happen to us?" Lucifer would have us doubt the Lord's love and "turn away." However, God is also a God of wisdom, and even godly love is tempered by wisdom. Too much concentration on the love of God exclusive of his wisdom presents opportunities to turn away a soul.

PUT GOD TO THE TEST

Because of the possibilities inherent in this type of thinking, the adversary is quite anxious to get us to put God to the test. He suggests that the Lord should prove His love for us by supplying some want or eliminating some sorrow. To a greater or lesser degree, practically all of us have faced this mist. When it happens in my own life, I find help in clearing it by saying to myself, "You are standing on the pinnacle of the temple. Don't jump!"

The Savior faced three major temptations after his forty-day fast. Satan suggested that He gratify His physical needs by turning stones to bread. Satan also offered all the power and riches of the world, and he tempted Jesus to throw himself from the pinnacle of the temple. In Luke's version of this event, the pinnacle temptation came last. Of the three temptations, the one that puzzled me the longest was jumping from the pinnacle. Why would the adversary want Jesus to jump? I could see how the first two temptations related to my own life, but what does jumping from a pinnacle have to do with me?

In the first two temptations, Jesus countered with scripture. "It is written," he said and then quoted a passage. Lucifer countered with his own knowledge of the scriptures: "If thou be the Son of God, cast thyself down from hence: For it is written, He shall give his angels charge over thee, to keep thee: And in their hands they shall bear thee up, lest at any time thou dash thy foot against a stone." (Luke 4:9–11.) "Since you have such faith in the scriptures and in your Father," Lucifer proposed, "since you claim to be His 'beloved' Son, put God to the test. How much faith do you really have in Him? If He truly loves you, He will catch you. He will not even allow your foot to stumble against a stone."

Jesus responded by quoting from the Old Testament. "Ye shall not tempt the Lord your God," Moses told the children of Israel, "as ye tempted him in Massah." (Deuteronomy 6:16.) *Massah* was the name Moses gave to the place where he brought water from the rock. In Hebrew it means "testing, trying, or proving." (Exodus 17:7, footnote a.) Before Moses brought the water from the rock, "the people did chide with Moses, and said, Give us water that we may drink. . . . Wherefore is this that thou hast brought us up out of Egypt, to kill us and our children and our cattle with thirst? . . . *They tempted the Lord, saying, Is the Lord among us, or not?*" (Exodus 17:2, 3, 7.)

In the minds of the people, God had to prove that He was with them. This proof would be seen in His taking care of all their needs. This was exactly what Satan was suggesting to Jesus in the wilderness. Jesus, however, did not put His Father to the test. He knew who He was, and He knew that His Father loved Him. He would not force His Father's hand. He backed away from the pinnacle. Unfortunately, in our own lives, sometimes we jump.

STANDING ON THE EDGE

Perhaps a few examples will help illustrate this mist. A couple I know wanted children badly and had not had any for many years. Finally they set a date. If the Lord really loved them, they would be pregnant by that date. The date came and passed without the desired pregnancy. Now the mists of doubt and the questions entered their minds. The opportunity for Satan to turn them away presented itself.

An active family who had been faithful all their lives faced a crisis when illness struck the mother. Fasts were called and prayers were offered. Her name was placed upon the prayer rolls of the temple. She received priesthood blessings. Surely God would not take this mother from her young children and grieving husband. God is all powerful. He is kind and merciful. He would surely hear the prayers and grant the desired healing. But the mother died.

In the last months of a mission, a hardworking elder and his companion wanted very much to baptize. They were working in a mission where few join the Church and many missionaries return home with only one or two baptisms. "If this is really the Lord's work and He cares about our success as missionaries," they thought, "we will baptize within the next months if we work our best." Lucifer always wants us to pin our faith upon the conditions we set, and he tries hard to make sure that we set conditions for God's love.

A DAY IN THE WILLOWS

When I was fourteen, I decided it was time I received my own testimony of the Book of Mormon. I began to read it, but as I read, I was filled with doubt about its truthfulness. I was frightened by my feelings, but I shared them with no one. One day after a particularly distressing day of reading, I decided to go into the willows by the river and pray until God gave me an answer. I begged God to take away the dark feelings and tell me if the Book of Mormon was true. "If you are really there and you love me, you will tell me," I prayed. For hours I stayed in the willows. Night came on, and yet I continued to pray. This had worked for Enos, so I prayed and prayed. Finally, hungry and cold, I left the willows and went to bed. I heard no voice. I felt no lightening of my load. I received no witness, no calm burning in the heart. I had demanded an answer on my terms, according to my time line, corresponding to my needs. I had jumped from the pinnacle.

Satan did not take Jesus to the pinnacle; the Spirit did. Neither did Satan take me into the willows. But the opportunity to turn away a soul was present. "God does not answer you because he is not listening to you, because you are not important to him," he whispered. This was a more powerful temptation at that time than, "God does not answer you because the Book of Mormon is false." Happily for me, there were enough previous witnesses to a Father in Heaven's love to counter the doubts. And my mother's faith in the Book of Mormon sustained me during the next years.

Please understand: It was right that I desired an answer. It was right that I prayed for it. It was right that I believed the promise God gave that He would grant me an answer. It was wrong to use the answer as a proof of His love. It was wrong in not allowing the Lord to choose His own time, place, and means for responding to my needs according to His wisdom. In all of the examples above, the prayers were right and proper; the danger of blinding mists comes in using the answers to those prayers as a test of God. There is a fine line between standing on the pinnacle with needing to jump to prove God's love and trusting that God will keep His promises without our making that fateful leap. We must say with Nephi, "I know that he loveth his children; nevertheless, I do not know the meaning of all things." (1 Nephi 11:17.) There may be times when we will fall from the pinnacle and God will need to catch us. There may be times when He will ask us in full faith to jump. But it is God's place to bring us to those moments, not ours. There may be times when He specifically asks us to "prove me now herewith" (Malachi 3:10), but those invitations are His to offer, not ours to demand.

Eventually I received my answer, and in a way and time that were far more powerful than I could ever have expected. God did not let my foot dash against the stone. I did not remain in doubt and darkness regarding the Book of Mormon. When we need water from the rock, we may ask for it, but we must not require that water as a proof of God's power or love, for then we are standing on the pinnacle responding to the tempter's voice that we must jump or forever remain in doubt. Can we not believe, as did Jesus, without casting ourselves down?

CHAPTER TWENTY

TALKING WITH
THE DONKEY

Various animals have become symbolic of certain character traits. The lion is known for majesty and courage, the ox for strength, the rooster for pride. The donkey is associated with foolish stubbornness. In a marvelous story in the Old Testament, the Lord used a donkey to show a man named Balaam his stubborn insistence on having his own way.

When the children of Israel finished their forty-year wandering and were camped on the east side of the Jordan River, the Moabites and Midianites were afraid of being overwhelmed by the invasion. But before trying to drive the Israelites away, they wanted a powerful prophet to make offerings to God and curse the Israelites. This type of sacrifice was common in the ancient world before going to war. The king of the Moabites, Balak, sought the services of Balaam, sending messengers promising to "promote [him] unto very great honour" and to enrich him with "the rewards of divination." (Numbers 22:17, 7.)

Balak's enticements were strong, and Balaam desired them, but before going he asked the Lord and received a plain answer: "Thou shalt not go with them; thou shalt not curse the people:

for they are blessed." (Numbers 22:12.) I don't see how the Lord could have been any plainer, even couching His answer in the language of command. Balaam gave this answer to the messengers who returned to Balak. Certain that he could persuade Balaam to come if he only made the rewards large enough, Balak sent new messengers with a higher offer. Balaam had already received a plain answer from the Lord, but he wanted the honors and wealth, so he told the messengers to stay the night and he would ask again.

What do we often do when we have received a plain answer but not one we wanted to hear? It is so natural to ask again and again until we get the answer we desire. There is a little bit of Balaam in all of us. This insistence often provides the tempter with opportunities. We must learn to bend our wishes to the wisdom of the Lord. Eager to teach Balaam a lesson, the Lord gave him permission to go, but He warned him not to do or say anything unless directed by the Lord himself. I also believe that the Lord saw Balaam's journey as an opportunity to supply future generations with a marvelous image to help them resist the tendency to make repeated demands. The image the Lord chose was Balaam's donkey. With the help of this animal, the Lord allowed Balaam to judge himself without realizing whom he was judging. Balaam would be given the opportunity to see himself as God saw him.

TURNING OUT OF THE WAY

As Balaam journeyed, content that the honors and rewards would now be his, the Lord sent an angel with a drawn sword to bar his way. However, only the donkey saw the barrier. "And the ass *turned aside out of the way*, and went into the field; and Balaam smote the ass, *to turn her into the way*." (Numbers 22:23.) If you've ridden a horse, you know how frustrating it can be when the horse will not go the way you want it to go. A donkey is usually even more obstinate. The wording of the scripture is interesting, for we are repeatedly advised not to turn from the strait and narrow way the Lord directs us to walk. How must He feel when, donkeylike, we strain against His guiding hands to go our own way?

The journey continued, and the angel "stood in a path of the vineyards, a wall being on this side, and a wall on that side. And . . . the ass . . . thrust herself unto the wall, and crushed Balaam's foot against the wall: and he smote her again." (Numbers 22:24–25.) Now there was no divergent path to walk. There were barriers on either side. There are also spiritual barriers placed to help keep us in the way we should go. How must the Lord feel when we thrust ourselves against those barriers?

The donkey saw the angel a third time. Again, the wording of the scriptures is interesting: "And the angel of the Lord went further, and stood in a narrow place, where was *no way to turn either to the right hand or to the left.*" (Numbers 22:26.) Throughout the scriptures we read these words in the context of obedience to the Lord's will. For example, the Lord instructed Joshua, "Observe to do according to all the law . . . : turn not from it to the right hand or to the left, that thou mayest prosper whithersoever thou goest." (Joshua 1:7.)

The donkey now "fell down under Balaam: and Balaam's anger was kindled, and he smote the ass with a staff." (Numbers 22:27.) If there is a cliché about donkeys, it has to do with their sitting down and stubbornly refusing to go forward. What a marvelous metaphor the Lord has supplied in this story for our own refusals to accept His will for us, go where He wants us to go, and allow Him to direct our paths.

At this point, "the Lord opened the mouth of the ass, and she said unto Balaam, What have I done unto thee, that thou hast smitten me these three times? And Balaam said unto the ass, Because *thou hast mocked me.*" (Numbers 22:28–29.) Balaam was rendering judgment on himself. God had allowed him to sit in the Lord's saddle, so to speak, and know what it is like to work with a recalcitrant person. In light of what finally happens to Balaam, it is easy to see that the counsel not to go was given for his own protection, not because the Lord was concerned that Balaam might curse Israel. Balaam had acted like a donkey. He had mocked the Lord. It was mockery because he asked the Lord for counsel, the Lord graciously gave it, but Balaam apparently had no intention of following it. With resignation Jesus once mildly scolded the people of his own generation by saying, "Why call ye me, Lord, Lord, and do not the things which I say?" (Luke 6:46.)

Like Balaam, many of us have a bit of a rebellious streak. We don't like to have our wills thwarted. Often our desires center around rewards of various kinds or the honors of men. At times we can even convince ourselves that our will really is the Lord's will. When we have created this mist for ourselves, it may be difficult to clear. I have found that humor is often effective in clearing certain mists. When I am tempted to turn to the right or to the left of the Lord's set path, or when, childlike, I collapse stubbornly in the road, refusing to go forward, I picture myself sitting on the road talking with Balaam's donkey. She often has a great deal of advice to give me. I can usually laugh at myself with that image in mind and then resist the urge to ask the Lord again for my desires, hoping He has changed His mind.

WASHING IN ABANA INSTEAD OF JORDAN

The best-known example of Balaam's lesson in modern times is the loss of the 116 pages of Book of Mormon manuscript. It is easy to discern from Joseph Smith's painful experience the type of mischief the adversary can create when we feel that our own way is better than the Lord's.

When Naaman, the leper, desired healing of Elisha, he was angry with the prophet's instructions: "I thought, He will surely come out to me, and stand, and call on the name of the Lord his God, and strike his hand over the place, and recover the leper. Are not Abana and Pharpar, rivers of Damascus, better than all the waters of Israel? May I not wash in them, and be clean? So he turned and went away in a rage." (2 Kings 5:11–12.) Like Balaam, Naaman had his own ideas. Only after he humbled himself enough to give up his preconceived expectations and accept the Lord's requests was the desired outcome granted. When the Lord has chosen the Jordan River for our cleansing, it makes no sense to insist on the Abana, but Lucifer will urgently support our feeling that we have a better idea.

As a new father I once asked my mother, who had reared my sisters and me alone, for her counsel on raising a righteous posterity. I was concerned about making some mistakes in my lack of experience. Her answer surprised me: "I decided very early that I was not smart enough to come up with a better plan than that of the Lord, so I did everything the prophets and apostles counseled me." My mother chose the Jordan instead of the Abana, and the results were according to the Lord's promises. Sometimes we accept the Lord's way as best for most people but think that we are an exception. There are, it is true, exceptions to almost every principle of the gospel, but they are much rarer than we would like to believe. If we feel that we are the exception to the Lord's commands; if we asked Him for counsel, and did not hear what we wanted; before returning to ask again, before turning to the left or right of the path, let us sit down and have a long conversation with Balaam's donkey. She may direct us away from some very painful mists.

CAMPING ON BALAK'S PEAKS

The Lord still allowed Balaam to continue his journey, but once again he warned him not to say or do anything not given him by the Lord. Balaam arrived in the land of Moab, much to Balak's delight. Now it was Balak's turn to teach us a great, supplementary lesson. "Balak took Balaam, and brought him up into the high places of Baal." (Numbers 22:41.) On the top of this mountain, Balaam built seven altars and offered sacrifice. The Spirit of the Lord descended upon Balaam, and he prophesied. But much to Balak's chagrin, the prophesy was all positive for the house of Israel: "From the top of the rocks I see him, and from the hills I behold him: lo, the people shall dwell alone, and shall not be reckoned among the nations. Who can count the dust of Jacob, and the number of the fourth part of Israel? Let me die the death of the righteous, and let my last end be like his!" (Numbers 23:9–10.)

Not willing to accept this blessing of Israel, Balak instructed Balaam to try again: "Come, I pray thee, with me unto another place, . . . and curse me them from thence." (Numbers 23:13.) Hoping for a different answer, Balak took Balaam "to the top of Pisgah, and built seven altars, and offered a bullock and a ram on every altar." (Numbers 23:14.) Once again the Spirit of the Lord fell upon Balaam, and he spoke the revealed will of God: "God is not a man, that he should lie; neither the son of man, that he should repent: hath he said, and shall he not do it? or hath he spoken, and shall he not make it good? Behold, I have received commandment to bless: and he hath blessed; and I cannot reverse it. . . . Surely there is no enchantment against Jacob, neither is there any divination against Israel." (Numbers 23:19–23.)

More frustrated than ever, and still unwilling to accept the Lord's answer, Balak encouraged Balaam to try again on another mountaintop, thinking that perhaps the place was not right. "Come, I pray thee, I will bring thee unto another place; peradventure it will please God that thou mayest curse me from thence. And Balak brought Balaam unto the top of Peor, that looketh toward Jeshimon." (Numbers 23:27–28.) The seven altars were built for a third time and the offerings made. But Balaam's answer was the same: "How goodly are thy tents,

O Jacob, and thy tabernacles, O Israel. . . . Blessed is he that blesseth thee, and cursed is he that curseth thee." (Numbers 24:5, 9.) Balaam then added a prophecy concerning the coming of the Savior, who would "rise out of Israel." (Numbers 24:17.)

THE BALAK IN US ALL

There is probably a lot of Balak in all of us. If we don't return again and again to the same person hoping for a different answer, we might run from person to person or from source to source until we find someone who will justify our preconceived assessment. Like Balak with his three different mountaintops, we find ourselves desperately searching for confirming evidence to support our position. Surely one of the mountaintops will bring the desired outcome. When I am tempted to do this, I say to myself, "Be careful; you are in danger of camping on Balak's peaks!"

A father in our stake related the following "camping on Balak's peaks" experience: "A few years ago, one of my daughters wanted the security of a steady boyfriend during her senior year in high school. Because she is a vivacious and pretty young woman, there were a few applicants willing to accommodate her. However, the counsel of the Church to the youth is to delay pairing off until the young man is home from a mission and the young woman is out of high school. This caused a certain amount of tension in our household. After numerous attempts to dissuade my daughter, I searched through the past speeches and writings of the presidents of the Church. I made a list of statements, including one from every Church president since David O. McKay. I felt fairly confident that this array of counsel would persuade her. She read the statements. I waited several days for her to respond. She returned to the discussion a few days later, having done a search of her own. She now showed me a *New Era* article written by a new member of the

Seventy. In the article he explained that he had married his high-school sweetheart. 'See,' my daughter said, 'even a General Authority steady-dated in high school, and look where he is now.' We finally reached a mutual compromise we both could live with, but I have never forgotten her look of triumph when she showed me her article."

I had to laugh as I reflected on this father's experience. From her vantage point on one of Balak's peaks, this young woman felt that her *New Era* article outweighed the list of statements made by Church presidents. I laughed, because I have camped on Balak's peaks enough times to recognize the strategy.

We are all familiar with the child who asks Dad for permission to do something, receives an unfavorable answer, and then swiftly goes to Mom, hoping for a different response. If we are not careful, we may find ourselves doing this with the scriptures. It is not too difficult, if we are willing to "wrest" the scriptures, to find a verse that will justify almost anything we want. We have probably all heard the scriptures quoted in some unjustified ways.

Camping on Balak's peaks may mean focusing on the words of former prophets rather than following the counsels of present ones. It may mean hearing the directions of a bishop and then going to the stake president, hoping for a new decision. Balak's peaks may pit the expertise of worldly wisdom against the revealed will of the Lord through His prophets. Sooner or later anyone can find a personal "soothsayer." Soothsayers say soothing sayings. They tell us what we want to hear. There is one on every peak in Balak's mountain range.

CHAPTER TWENTY-ONE

TIE A KNOT
AND HANG ON

When I was in elementary school, we were expected to climb a rope to the top of the gym. Since our muscles were not greatly developed, the instructor had tied a knot in the rope about halfway up. If we could just climb high enough, we could reach the knot and stand on it while we caught our breath. In this manner we eventually reached the top. The knot was our lifesaver. Someone once gave me some good advice about trial and temptation, and I think of that knot every time I remember his words: "When you get to the end of your rope, tie a knot and hang on." This was his way of saying that I must not give in or give up no matter how spiritually exhausted I became, for in time, the trial would end or the temptation cease. Since I did not know how soon the relief would come, and since to stop fighting meant defeat, the only intelligent thing to do was "just hang on."

I have learned in life that one of Lucifer's mists is the suggestion that relief will never come, and that we are justified in giving in or giving up because we have already fought so long and hard. Sometimes Satan suggests that God does not love us or surely He would have rescued us long ago. If we are waiting for an expected blessing, he might whisper that it is not worth the wait, and that we can have at least a measure of happiness by settling for a lesser objective. These are the times we must tie a knot in the rope and hang on.

The scriptures show numerous examples of those who gave in just as they neared the end of their trials. These are tragic moments when viewed with hindsight, but they are important in their instruction for all of us.

THIRTY-FOURTH YEAR, FIRST MONTH, FOURTH DAY

I can think of no greater blessing that could come to a people than the one that came to the Nephites and Lamanites who witnessed the ministry of Christ as related in third Nephi. But there were those who missed it, and by only a few years. Before the Savior's visit, the people had been on a roller-coaster ride from the heights of righteousness to the depths of iniquity. After a close brush with destruction because of the strength of the Gadianton robbers, the entire nation repented, completely turning to the Lord. Mormon gives us a detailed description of the people at this time:

"Their hearts were swollen with joy, unto the gushing out of many tears, because of the great goodness of God in delivering them out of the hands of their enemies; and *they knew* it was because of their repentance and their humility. . . . And now behold, there was not a living soul among all the people of the Nephites who did doubt in the least the words of all the holy prophets who had spoken; for *they knew* that it must needs be that they must be fulfilled. And *they knew* that it must be expedient that Christ had come. . . . Therefore they did forsake all their sins, and their abominations, and their whoredoms, and did serve God with all diligence day and night." (3 Nephi 4:33–5:4.)

Mormon tells us that this was the state of the people in the year A.D. 21. We know that the great destruction immediately before the appearance of Christ in the Americas took place "in the thirty and fourth year, in the first month, on the fourth day." (3 Nephi 8:5.) If the people could just maintain their righteousness for thirteen years, they would be part of the wonderful events that took place during the ministry of Jesus. From this time on, Mormon gives us a yearly description of the spiritual state of the people. Let us see how close they get to the greatest blessing of the Book of Mormon.

Immediately following his previous description, Mormon advances us to the twenty-fifth year: "And thus had the twenty and second year passed away, and the twenty and third year also, and the twenty and fourth, and the twenty and fifth." (3 Nephi 5:7.) As the twenty-fifth year passed, the people were only eight years away from the Savior's visit. The next two years are described by Mormon in these words: "And they began again to prosper and to wax great; and the twenty and sixth and seventh years passed away, and there was *great order in the land;* and they had *formed their laws according to equity and justice.* And now *there was nothing in all the land to hinder* the people from prospering continually, except they should fall into transgression." (3 Nephi 6:4–5.) They now just needed to maintain their righteousness for six more years. I can almost see the angels in heaven cheering them on.

Mormon tells us that the next year was spent in building cities and highways. "And thus passed away the twenty and eighth year, and the people had continual peace." (3 Nephi 6:9.) They had reached the five-year point, with the Savior's visit just around the corner. Five more years of righteousness, and the victory was theirs. Unfortunately, the twenty-ninth year proved to be their undoing.

"But it came to pass in the twenty and ninth year there began to be some disputings among the people; and some were lifted up into pride and boastings because of their exceedingly great riches." (3 Nephi 6:10.) This pride led to "many merchants . . . , many lawyers, . . . and many officers. And the people began to be distinguished by ranks. . . . And thus there became a great inequality in all the land, insomuch that the church began to be broken up." (3 Nephi 6:11–14.) "In the commencement of the thirtieth year—the people [were] carried about by the temptations of the devil whithersoever he desired to carry them, and to do whatsoever iniquity he desired they should." (3 Nephi 6:17.) In the thirty-first year the government was destroyed, and the people were broken up into tribes.

They came so close and paid such a terrible price for letting the rope slip from their hands. Not only did they miss the Savior's visit, but they also suffered the destructions described in third Nephi. We never know what is just around the corner; and what a tragedy it is when a blessing is so close and we give up just a little too soon. What a painful awakening it must have been for the wicked Nephites who, on the other side of the veil, realized how close they had come and what a wonderful experience they had missed.

Mormon relates one important detail about the year just before the destructive storm and following visit of Christ. Nephi, the leader of the church, "did cry unto the people in the commencement of the thirty and third year; and he did preach unto them repentance and remission of sins. . . . And there were many in the commencement of this year that were baptized unto repentance; and thus the more part of the year did pass away." (3 Nephi 7:23, 26.)

How must those people—who hearkened unto Nephi, repented, and therefore were not destroyed but were part of the wonderful events marking Christ's ministry—have felt as they reflected on how close they had come to missing that blessing. What if they had not changed? What if they had delayed their repentance just one more year? We can imagine their gratitude and joy as they reflected on the past year's events.

SAUL'S TRAGIC IMPATIENCE

The story of Saul in the Old Testament is perhaps even more tragic, for he let go of the rope just minutes before the relief he sought came. Saul faced a coming battle with the Philistines and needed to offer the required sacrifices. He had received word from Samuel that he would meet him to make the offering. His own people were fearful and began to "hide themselves in caves, and in thickets, and in rocks, and in high places, and in pits. And some of the Hebrews went over Jordan. . . . As for Saul, he was yet in Gilgal, and all the people followed him trembling." (1 Samuel 13:6–7.) Saul was certainly in a precarious position. He needed to attack soon or his army would melt away, but Samuel had not yet arrived, and the offerings were yet to be made. Saul "tarried seven days, according to the set time that Samuel had appointed: but Samuel came not to Gilgal; and the people were scattered from him." (1 Samuel 13:8.)

What should he do? The pressure to act grew intense, but instead of tying the knot at the end of his rope and hanging on a little while longer, Saul decided to offer the sacrifices himself. Had he not been anointed king over the people? Did he not, therefore, have as much authority as Samuel? "And Saul said, Bring hither a burnt offering to me, and peace offerings. And he offered the burnt offering." (1 Samuel 13:9.) Saul had assumed an authority he did not possess, and in making the offering he offended the very God whose help he sought, but the foolishness of his decision was immediately revealed.

"And it came to pass, that *as soon as he had made an end of offering the burnt offering, behold, Samuel came;* and . . . said, What hast thou done? And Saul said, Because I saw that the people were scattered from me, and that thou camest not within the days appointed, and that the Philistines gathered themselves together at Michmash: Therefore . . . I forced myself . . . and offered a burnt offering." (1 Samuel 13:10–12.)

Saul had many good reasons for not waiting, but the fact remains that he failed the test, and by just a few moments. "And Samuel said to Saul, Thou hast done foolishly: thou hast not kept the commandment of the Lord thy God, . . . for now would the Lord have established thy kingdom upon Israel forever. But now thy kingdom shall not continue: the Lord hath sought him a man after his own heart." (1 Samuel 13:13–14.)

This one moment was pivotal in the life of King Saul. From that time on his humility and spirituality diminished. The history of the house of Israel would have been vastly different but for a few minutes of time.

JUST A FEW HOURS MORE . . .

I recall a time when I witnessed a situation similar to those described in the scriptures. I was teaching seminary and became friends with a young woman we will call Jennifer. She was not very popular, considered herself plain, and rarely dated. Her family was not very active, but she did the best she could to live the gospel fully. Her attendance at seminary was excellent, and I was very fond of her.

There was a wonderful young man who took the same seminary class as she did. We will call him Gary. He was kind to Jennifer. Every parent would be honored to have a son like this young man. He had one problem, however; he was extremely shy. Though he was good looking and came from an active family, he dated rarely. I was also very close to him.

Both Jennifer and Gary had on separate occasions confided in me that they liked each other, but they swore me to secrecy about their feelings. The big dance of the year was approaching, and Gary wanted very much to take Jennifer, but he was afraid she would turn him down. I kept assuring him that his chances were very good, but his shyness remained a problem.

At this stage another young man entered the picture. We will call him John. John was very confident with the young women. He was popular on campus and well known. His morals, however, were not very high. He was the type of young man that would make a young woman's parents feel nervous. For some reason he started paying attention to Jennifer. This was flattering to her but also a concern. She came into my office one day to talk about him. Aware of the conflict she was struggling with, I urged Gary even more earnestly to ask Jennifer to the dance. I felt that if he asked her, it would give her the sense of worth she needed to avoid John. I finally convinced Gary, and he promised to ask her out on Friday. Thursday afternoon, John asked her to the dance. She did not agree to go, but told him she would call that evening. Once again she came to the office.

"Would it be such a bad thing to go with John?" she asked. "I've never been to a big dance. I've never worn a corsage or been to a nice dinner or worn a prom dress. This is my senior year, my last chance, and yet I don't feel right about going with him."

"Maybe someone else will ask you," I suggested, knowing who would call in just a few hours.

"No one else will ask me," she replied. "This is my only chance."

"You never know what is just around the corner," I offered. "Besides, if you feel uncomfortable, perhaps it would be better not to go at all."

She thanked me for listening to her, told me she would think it over, and left. That evening she phoned John and accepted his invitation. In a small town word travels fast, and the next morning Gary heard that Jennifer was going with John. The date came and went. From that time on John spent more and more time with Jennifer. I tried to talk Gary into asking her out, but he answered, "She's John's girlfriend."

I watched Jennifer go downhill through the rest of the year. Her attendance began to slip. I thought if she could go away to school things might turn around again. With the help of the school we were able to arrange a scholarship for her, since her grades were good. This was to be announced after seminary graduation. However, her bishop phoned me one evening to tell me that Jennifer would not be graduating. I didn't ask why, but it soon became known that she was going to have a baby, and Jennifer and John were married at the end of the school year. Their activity in the Church is minimal.

I have thought since how close she came to dating the finest boy in the community. If I had known what was going to happen, I would have told her that afternoon that she was just a few hours away from a phone call from the boy she liked best. I never told her those things, and to this day she does not know. I am not suggesting that she would have married Gary and lived happily ever after, but I have the conviction that had she been able to hold firm to her standards one more day, her whole life could have been different. Since we do not know what is around the corner, or how soon the blessings we seek may come, or when the test will end, we must not allow ourselves to be blinded by the mist that tells us the corner will never come.

"THE CORNER WASN'T SO FAR AWAY"

I have also seen things turn out another way. While teaching at BYU, I became close to a young woman who was in love with a young man from her home state who was not a member of the Church. Her parents hoped that if she attended BYU, perhaps she would forget the boy back home and find a Latter-day Saint she could marry. She was unhappy and homesick throughout the semester, and in spite of all efforts to dissuade her, she decided to leave BYU and attend a local college in her home state. She felt sure that if she married the boy back home, she could eventually convert him to the Church.

I remember our conversation the last day of the semester. I urged her to think seriously about the future, to stay at least the full year at the Y. "Perhaps you will meet someone here that will be as wonderful as the boy back home," I said. "No one will ever be that great," she replied. I watched her leave with anxiety for her future. The winter semester passed as well as the spring and summer terms. To my surprise she walked into my office the first week of class the following fall semester.

She had tried to convert her boyfriend, failed, and somehow, with the help of good parents, found the courage to end the relationship. She returned to school as dejected and discouraged a young woman as you could meet. I told her, "You never know what is just around the corner. Tie a knot in your rope and hang on." She didn't believe me, but within two years she had met another young man who was worthy to marry her in the temple. I was able to attend that marriage. After the ceremony, she whispered to me in the sealing room, "My knot held, and the corner wasn't so far away, was it?"

SIX-DIP SAINTS

As a Primary child I learned and loved the story of Naaman, the Syrian leper, who was told by Elisha, "Wash in Jordan seven times, and thy flesh shall come again to thee, and thou shalt be clean." (2 Kings 5:10.) Though angry at first because Elisha did not meet him personally and ask him to accomplish some great feat, eventually he went "down, and dipped himself seven times in Jordan, according to the saying of the man of God: and his flesh came again like unto the flesh of a little child." (2 Kings 5:14.)

I wonder why Elisha asked Naaman to dip seven times in the Jordan. Why not wash just once? What did Naaman think as he arose from the first bath and looked at his skin to see if the prophet's instructions were working? What were his thoughts with each successive immersion? What would have happened had he given up at the sixth washing, allowing his initial anger to return, believing he was wasting his time?

I used to think the seventh washing was the one that did the trick, but I believe now it was the sum of all seven trips to the river that brought the promised blessing. There are a multiplicity of simple things we are asked to do by the Lord. So often it is the accumulation of repeated simple actions that over time bring the results. I have found this to be true in such areas as understanding the scriptures, learning the truths in the symbols of the temple, strengthening my relationship with my family, and paying tithing. We all need more patience than we possess. When we arise from the fifth and sixth dipping, we must not lose hope or give in. Let us persevere until the seventh washing, when all the promises of the Lord are fulfilled. Lucifer would have us be six-dip Saints, but the Lord assures us the blessing comes after that seventh washing.

All of life can be viewed from this perspective. Though it seems long to us, in the light of eternity, we experience mortality as the blink of an eye. David understood this and wrote, "As for man, his days are as grass: as a flower of the field, so he flourisheth. For the wind passeth over it, and it is gone; and the place thereof shall know it no more." (Psalm 103:15–16.) And Jacob concluded his record with, "The time passed away with us, and also our lives passed away like as it were unto us a dream." (Jacob 7:26.)

We have the promise that if we pass this mortal test and are readmitted into the presence of our Father in Heaven, we will "go no more out." (Revelation 3:12.) I remember as a boy the exhilaration I felt when school was out for the year and vacation began. During the last months of the school year, I looked forward to that glorious feeling of liberation, and it sustained me. I needed to work at my studies just a little longer. I knew what was just around the corner in June. Perhaps, in a small measure, that feeling is but a shadow of what is to come when the schooling of our life is completed. What is true of individual moments in our lives is true of all of life. Let us dip all seven times; and when our faith seems tried to the breaking point, let us tie the knot in the end of the rope and hang on.

CHAPTER TWENTY-TWO

THE HARD SAYINGS

According to many places in the scriptures, the main challenge in life is to stay on a path that is described as strait and narrow. In Lehi's dream, Satan's goal is to obscure that path with the mists of darkness. The Savior's life teaches us two major defenses against leaving that path. Immediately after Jesus fed the five thousand, He went to Capernaum. Those He had fed the previous day found Him in the synagogue. They had witnessed His power and wanted Him to be their king and continue to take care of their temporal needs. This included everything from miraculous meals to freedom from the Romans. Their focus was their physical needs, but Jesus had come to take care of their spiritual ones.

In a powerful speech known as the Discourse on the Bread of Life, Jesus tried to tell them that He could not be the kind of Messiah they wanted. He had to be the kind of Savior they needed—the kind His Father had commanded Him to be. This went against so many of their traditions and expectations that they were offended, murmuring, "This is an hard saying; who can hear it?" (John 6:60.)

Jesus answered by intimating that there might be even

harder ones down the road. It was, therefore, necessary for them to learn to see His mission as spiritual rather than temporal. This was too much for many of His followers: "From that time many of his disciples went back, and walked no more with him." (John 6:66.)

TODAY'S HARD SAYINGS

Along the path will be many "hard sayings" we will be asked to accept and act upon. These sayings are different for each of us. There is no need to judge each other. My hard saying may be very easy for others, and theirs may present no difficulties for me. For some young men, "Every worthy young man should fill a mission" may be a hard saying. The call for more older couples in the mission field may present a fearful challenge to many. Tithing is a hard saying for more members of the Church than we may realize. To some women, the counsel to come home from the workplace may be a hard saying. The youth may find the standards of the Church in *For the Strength of Youth* a major limit to their desires. Certain trials, disappointments, or calls to leadership may constitute hard sayings for other. The list could go on and on. I doubt that any of us will reach the end of the path without facing a few hard sayings.

These moments present Lucifer with the opportunity to get us to do what the disciples of Jesus did—to walk no more with Him. He would have us see the path as so strait and narrow that it hardly has room for us. At that point he uses a deceptive mist to get us off the Lord's path. He suggests there are other paths that will get us where we want to go. But we must not be deceived.

"WILL YE ALSO GO AWAY?"

When the synagogue was emptied, Jesus stood alone with his twelve faithful apostles. In a poignant moment He turned to them and asked, "Will ye also go away? Then Simon Peter answered him, Lord, *to whom shall we go? Thou hast the words of eternal life.*" (John 6:67–68.)

In one sentence, Peter dispelled the mist that leads so many others away from the path when the hard sayings come. He knew there was no other path! He could, therefore, fully commit to the one laid out by the Savior. When we realize there is no other path, we take a deep breath and move forward, facing our hard sayings, largely because there is no alternative.

The scriptures give many titles for the Savior. He is the Bread of Life, the Living Water, the Light, the Way, the Truth, the Good Shepherd, the True Vine, the Rock, and so on. When He offers the bread of life to the world, many say, "I can see that this is good bread, but it is not quite to my liking. I will partake of other bread more suitable to my palate." As these people turn to go, the Savior whispers, "*There is no other bread.*" To those who would rather not gather with his flock, preferring other shepherds, he cries, "*There is no other shepherd.*" For those who seek another, easier path that does not limit them so much or climb so steeply, he warns, "*There is no other path.*"

THERE COULD BE NO LIGHT AT ALL

This idea was dramatically taught to the Nephites during the three days of darkness. Mormon, when writing his description of that darkness, wanted to make sure we realize there was no other source of light at all. The darkness was complete: "And *there could be no light,* because of the darkness, neither candles, neither torches; neither could there be fire kindled with their fine and exceedingly dry wood, so that *there could be no light at all;* and there was *not any light seen,* neither fire, nor glimmer, neither the sun, nor the moon, nor the stars, for so great were the mists of darkness which were upon the face of the land. And it came to pass that it did last for the space of three days that *there was no light seen.*" (3 Nephi 8:21–23.)

The Lord was teaching those who were not destroyed what

life is like without the Savior. We can choose to be in God's light or wander forever through the mists of darkness, but there is no other light. This was emphasized when, through the mists of darkness, the voice of the Savior was heard, saying, "I am the *light and the life* of the world." (3 Nephi 9:18.) We can imagine the impact that statement would have on those sitting in the blackness after having attempted to see or create another source of light. *There is no other light!*

"THERE IS NO OTHER STREAM"

In the *Chronicles of Narnia*, C. S. Lewis taught this same principle. In these children's stories, the great lion, Aslan, is a symbolic representation of the Savior, and they should be read with that truth in mind. In the quotation below, Jill, a new visitor to the land of Narnia, Aslan's kingdom, is wandering in a wood. She is thirsty and hears the sound of a stream in the distance. She heads in the direction of the stream, her thirst increasing. When she finds it, however, she stops, for there next to its bank sits a great lion.

> "Are you not thirsty?" said the Lion.
> "I am dying of thirst," said Jill.
> "Then drink," said the Lion. . . .
> "Will you promise not to—do anything to me, if I do come?" said Jill.
> "I make no promise," said the Lion.
> Jill was so thirsty now that, without noticing it, she had come a step nearer.
> "Do you eat girls?" she said.
> "I have swallowed up girls and boys, women and men, kings and emperors, cities and realms," said the Lion. It didn't say this as if it were boasting, nor as if it were sorry, nor as if it were angry. It just said it.
> "I daren't come and drink," said Jill.
> "Then you will die of thirst," said the Lion.

"Oh dear!" said Jill, coming another step nearer. "I suppose I must go and look for another stream then."

"There is no other stream," said the Lion. (*The Silver Chair* [New York: Collier Books, 1970], pp. 16–17.)

There is no other stream. We must drink or die. We must walk his path or be forever lost. We must feast on his bread or starve. We must see by his light or wander hopelessly in the darkness. We must build on his rock or forever feel the shifting sands beneath our feet. This is the one truth about the path that Satan desperately wants to hide.

"ONLY ONE WAY TO GET TO HEAVEN"

I once asked a young boy graduating from Primary what was his favorite scripture story. "The Tower of Babel," he quickly responded. His answer was somewhat of a shock for me, so I asked him what that story taught him. "It teaches me that there is only one way to get to heaven—righteousness," he said. We cannot build our own stairway to heaven; we must climb the one the Lord has provided. Lest we be deceived, that way is quickly described in Genesis, where we read of Jacob's dream of a ladder or stairway reaching into heaven. This stairway is constructed by the Lord, for He stands above it waiting for His children to climb toward Him. Far too many people want to build their own stairway, and though they may proceed with their construction plans, they never reach high enough to achieve the goal of reunion with our Father in Heaven. There is no other stair!

CARRY THE CROSS

Just before His transfiguration, Jesus began to teach His apostles "that he must go unto Jerusalem, and suffer many things of the elders and chief priests and scribes, and be killed, and be raised again the third day." (Matthew 16:21.) As we can imagine, this was distressing news to His disciples. With the best of intentions, I am sure, Peter offered the Savior his reaction to this announcement: "Then Peter took him, and began to rebuke him, saying, Be it far from thee, Lord: this shall not be unto thee." The suggestion that He need not fulfill His Father's will, even though given by Peter in innocence and lack of understanding, brought a severe response from the Savior: "Get thee behind me, Satan: thou art an offence unto me: for thou savourest not the things that be of God, but those that be of men." (Matthew 16:22–23.)

The Savior had to walk the path like everyone else. His path contained a few hard sayings also. As He looked up the length of His path, he saw a cup, a crown of thorns, and a cross. He knew that He had to drink that cup, wear that crown, and carry that cross. Suddenly a man, a friend, stood on the path between Him and His cross suggesting that He need not pick it up. "Get behind me," He replied. "Don't tempt me to think I do not need to walk the path my Father has asked me to walk. When you do this, you offend me. You are not thinking of the things of God; you are thinking like a man."

Jesus then applied this same standard to all of us: "If any man will come after me, let him deny himself, and take up his cross and follow me." The Joseph Smith Translation adds the following explanation: "And now for a man to take up his cross, is to deny himself all ungodliness, and every worldly lust, and keep my commandments." (JST, Matthew 16:26.)

SAVORING THE THINGS OF GOD

The Savior has asked us to imagine our own path stretching out in front of us. Along its length, just as there was on His, there will be some crosses to bear, some hard sayings to face. Once again, I emphasize that these crosses may be different for each of us. You may find my cross easy to pick up, even though for me it is a heavy burden. We will not judge each other in these matters.

As we face our crosses, often some well-intentioned friend stands in front of us on the path, reassuring us that we don't need to pick this one up. We may also find ourselves on the path of others, telling them they need not deny some ungodliness, or conquer some worldly lust, or keep some minor commandment. Well-intentioned though we may be, we may inadvertently be helping the adversary to spread his mists, for he will always be the first to suggest that we need not face our crosses. Did not Jesus address Peter as "Satan," meaning that he had become his tempter, his adversary.

When such moments come, we must kindly, tactfully, firmly, and lovingly tell those standing in our way to get behind us: "Please don't suggest that I don't have to carry a cross my Father has placed in my path. When you do this, you are offending me. You are thinking as a man, not as God."

We would be more useful to one another if we would help each other pick up the crosses of our lives. It is a rule of life that those who encourage us to obey the Lord are our true friends, just as those who suggest that we need not obey, for the moment at least, are our foes.

When teenagers are tempted to date before age sixteen, there will often be friends who can give good reasons why the counsel does not apply. When the most popular movie of the day does not meet LDS standards, we can usually find someone to give us good reasons to see it anyway. When the young man wavers in his commitment to serve a mission, someone may advise that he is an exception to the rule. When a young woman wishes to marry outside the temple, friends may assure her that all will be well in the long run. How could the Church try to prevent her from marrying a man she loves? When a young mother is offered a job that will bring many desired things to her family, inevitably some can provide excellent reasons why she should take it.

Let us remember the encounter between Peter and the

Savior. Let us keep in our minds a clear vision of the path before us and never allow another to stand between us and the crosses we are asked to bear. Then, as Jacob taught, we will find an eternal reward awaiting us when we reach our destination: "Behold, the righteous, the saints of the Holy One of Israel, they who have believed in the Holy One of Israel, they who have *endured the crosses of the world,* and despised the shame of it, they shall inherit the kingdom of God, which was prepared for them from the foundation of the world, *and their joy shall be full forever.*" (2 Nephi 9:18.)

CHAPTER TWENTY-THREE

TROUBLING THE CAMP OF ISRAEL

Sometimes when people are defending behaviors or decisions that are wrong or dangerous, they say, "It's my life and I can do with it what I want. I'm only hurting myself." We can be fairly confident that those who believe this justification are blinded by a mist. In Lehi's dream, the adversary was most eager that we not see the river, which represents the consequences, the misery, that people fall into when they stray from the path. Usually that misery engulfs others.

There is no action or decision that we make that will not in time affect another human being. Our lives are so intricately linked that, for good or for ill, our actions have profound consequences on others. Lucifer would have us deny this truth. There is evidence of this from the earliest stages of history. When asked about his brother Abel, Cain replied, "Am I my brother's keeper?" (Moses 5:34.)

We clear this mist, and thus are able to make better choices, when we accept the responsibility of our actions, both in their consequences for ourselves and for those around us. As is true with most mists, the scriptures include many examples to give us a clearer vision.

ACHAN'S TRANSGRESSION

When Joshua was commanded to conquer Jericho, the Lord specifically warned the people not to take any spoils for themselves: "In any wise keep yourselves from the accursed thing, lest ye make yourselves accursed, when ye take of the accursed thing, *and make the camp of Israel a curse, and trouble it.*" (Joshua 6:18.) "Accursed" in these instructions means that which is banned or set aside, the opposite of consecrated. The Lord was plain in His instructions. If a single person took the spoils, all of Israel would be "troubled."

When the walls fell, everyone followed the Lord's wishes except Achan. He could not resist helping himself to "a goodly Babylonish garment, and two hundred shekels of silver, and a wedge of gold of fifty shekels weight." (Joshua 7:21.) These he hid in the earth under his tent. Since no one knew of his deed, he felt safe. No one knew except the Lord. The next city Joshua was asked to conquer was Ai. It was such a small town that he did not feel it necessary to send the whole army. He sent three thousand soldiers. The attack was a disaster. The men of Ai defeated Joshua's force, killed thirty-six of his men, and chased the remainder down the hills. This was distressing news for the rest of the people. If such a small town could defeat them, how could they ever hope to drive out the rest of the Canaanites? "Wherefore the hearts of the people melted, and became as water." (Joshua 7:5.)

"Joshua rent his clothes, and fell to the earth upon his face before the ark of the Lord." (Joshua 7:6.) Why had the Lord commanded them to win the land if He was not going to help them? What would happen when the other cities learned that a small force could turn the Israelite army?

"And the Lord said unto Joshua, Get thee up; wherefore liest thou thus upon thy face? Israel hath sinned, and they have also transgressed my covenant which I commanded them: for they have even taken of the accursed thing, and have also stolen. . . . Therefore the children of Israel could not stand before their enemies . . . : neither will I be with you any more, except ye destroy the accursed from among you." (Joshua 7:10–11.)

At first reading this hardly seems fair. Not all of Israel disobeyed, but only one man and his family. The thirty-six men who died in battle were righteous. Why should all suffer because of the rebellion of one man? It appears that the Lord wanted the people to learn how important it was for the entire nation that each individual remain true. All would be affected by the actions of every member. The situation with Achan was used as an example, a strong example, to make sure the people were not blinded by thinking, "It's my life. I'm only hurting myself." If the people, through the example of Achan, rejected this mist of Satan, they would have strong motivation to choose righteousness.

"THAT MAN PERISHED NOT ALONE"

Achan was eventually discovered and punished, but the memory of his action remained fresh in the people's minds. The Lord's wisdom in the Achan affair became quickly apparent.

Two and a half of the twelve tribes wanted to live on the east side of the Jordan River. This desire was granted, but it presented a problem for these tribes. The Jordan River Valley is extremely deep. The hills climb steeply from the river's banks on both sides. With such a natural barrier to separate them, the two and a half tribes feared that in time the other tribes would reject their children. To remind those on both sides of the river that they belonged to each other, the tribes on the east decided to build an altar by the bank of the river.

The tribes on the west side of the river misunderstood the intentions of their fellow Israelites. They believed they had built the altar to one of the Canaanite gods. They gathered an army to root out this evil before they all suffered, but before they attacked, they sent a delegation consisting of a prince from every tribe to explain why they were coming to attack. "Thus saith the whole congregation of the Lord, What trespass is this that ye have committed against the God of Israel, to turn away this day from following the Lord, in that ye have builded you an altar, that ye might rebel to day against the Lord? . . . And it will be, seeing ye rebel to day against the Lord, *that to morrow he will be wroth with the whole congregation of Israel. . . . Did not Achan . . . commit a trespass in the accursed thing, and wrath fell on all the congregation of Israel? and that man perished not alone in his iniquity.*" (Joshua 22:16–20.)

"FITLY JOINED TOGETHER"

This principle works both ways. Our righteous actions also have an impact far beyond ourselves. Lucifer would also blind us to the importance of each person's contribution. In the Doctrine and Covenants, the Lord explained His many spiritual gifts and affirmed that "to every man is given a gift by the Spirit of God." (D&C 46:11.) The Lord does not want a single member of His Church to feel unimportant because the ward or stake could get along fine without that member's help. Each baptized member has a gift. It may be the gift of healing, of discernment, of wisdom or knowledge or faith. All are necessary. Each provides valuable blessings and assistance to the other members of the Church. Paul explained this principle by comparing the individual members of the Church to a body, which is "fitly joined together and compacted by that *which every joint supplieth,* . . . making increase of the body unto the edifying of itself in love." (Ephesians 4:16.) The realization of this truth clears a mist that often darkens the path of the less active.

When I was about seven years old, we built a new chapel in my hometown. In those days much of the labor for a new building was supplied by the local wards. My mother took me to the building site while she helped with the construction. I wandered from place to place watching the workmen. Our bishop saw me, took me by the hand, and led me into the chapel. He gave me a small can of putty and a putty knife. The workmen had just finished putting up oak panels on the sides of the chapel.

"Do you see all the little nail holes in this beautiful wood?" the bishop asked me. "I want you to fill them up." He showed me how to put a tiny bit of putty on the edge of the knife, press it into a sunken nail hole, and then scrape it smooth. He watched me for a while until I knew how to do it correctly. Then he left to attend to other concerns.

For hours I filled the nail holes. I felt so important and needed. I was helping the Lord build His church. When I was finished with both sides of the chapel, I showed my mother what I had done. Every time I entered the chapel, I looked at the oak paneling and felt a sense of belonging. This feeling continued into my teenage years and then into adulthood. Thirty years later, I could still remember the warm pride of contributing to building up Zion. When they finally covered the oak paneling a few years ago with a new wall covering, I felt a sense of loss. I could no longer run my finger over the nail holes I had filled in so many years ago.

What is true of my feelings as a child is true of every calling or act of service we do in the Church. We are contributing to others. Our actions do count. When we are absent, we are missed. But the adversary would have us think we are not important, that it is our life, and that our absence hurts only ourselves.

I was interested recently in a comment made by a father to his son. The son was raised by his mother after a divorce when he was only a little child. After trying to explain to his father the impact his absence had had on the family, the father replied, "I didn't think I mattered that much because your mother was so capable. I never realized I was missed."

A MORE DISTANT VISION

Perhaps the most tragic consequences of thinking, "It's my life and I'm only hurting myself," are those that fall upon our families, especially our children and grandchildren. I believe that the most important lesson taught by Laman and Lemuel centers on their descendants. When Lehi gave his final blessings to his children, he turned to the sons and daughters of Laman and Lemuel, his grandchildren, in sorrow.

"Behold, my sons and my daughters," he said to them, "I cannot go down to my grave save I should leave a blessing upon you; for behold, I know that if ye are brought up in the way ye should go ye will not depart from it. Wherefore, if ye are cursed, behold, I leave my blessing upon you, that the cursing may be taken from you and be answered upon the heads of your parents." (2 Nephi 4:5–6.)

It is important when we make decisions that we see how those actions will affect not only those around us but also the unborn generations that have yet to experience mortal probation. We may be choosing for them. In the case of Laman and Lemuel, their choice of resistance to the Lord's will lasted through five hundred years of their descendants. They made a choice for hundreds of thousands. They might have said, "It's my life and I'm only hurting myself," but they believed in a lie, one of the greatest lies of mankind.

YOUR FAMILY OR YOUR FAITH

These more distant consequences of our actions are so important to understand. Those who marry a nonmember or inactive member need to realize that their decision will affect hundreds of descendants. On the other hand, those who join the Church and devote their life to its principles are making a decision that will affect for good the lives of hundreds of descendants. We simply must see through the mist that would obscure that more distant vision.

My ancestor Anders Jensen watched some boys in a street in Copenhagen who were beating up another boy because he was a Latter-day Saint. He went to help him, and they became friends. The boy gave him a tract containing the story of Joseph Smith. Believing in the Restoration, he tried to convince his family. They rejected his testimony, which brought a crisis in his life. If he joined the Church, they would cut him off from the family. "You must choose between your family and your faith," he was told.

He chose his faith and never saw his family again. For years as I listened to that story, I wondered how he could make such a choice, since family is such a precious thing. I finally realized that in an ironic manner he really chose his family along with his faith—he chose for his future family. As he walked away from his home on that day, perhaps he thought of his descendants seven and eight generations in the future. I like to believe that he chose for us, and that his distant vision, which included our profound gratitude, gave him the strength to do what he had to do—what was right to do.

"A PERFECT KNOWLEDGE"

The prophet Jacob spoke of a future judgment when "we shall have a *perfect knowledge* of *all* our guilt, and our uncleanness, and our nakedness; and the righteous shall have a *perfect knowledge* of their enjoyment, and their righteousness, being clothed with purity, yea, even with the robe of righteousness." (2 Nephi 9:14.)

What constitutes a "perfect knowledge" of guilt or righteousness? I wonder if it does not include the knowledge of how our actions have affected the lives of others. We do not always know in this life how far our influence reaches. Like the circles on a pond when we throw in a pebble, our actions flow outward. What sorrow may we feel when the mists are pulled away and we see the problems and misery we may have brought upon another child of God? On the other hand, what joy and peace may overwhelm us as we understand the nobility and goodness we have fostered in others and as we hear their expressions of gratitude?

CHAPTER TWENTY-FOUR

SHEDDING ESAU'S TEARS

We have all seen many tears throughout our lives. They come from different people in many different situations. Those from family members or close friends are often the most painful to witness. But I think the most troubling of all are Esau's tears.

One of the stories I've learned the most from is that of Esau. He is not a major character in the Bible, but he has a critical message to tell us about the mists that allow us to see only our immediate desires while blinding us to future awakenings.

SELLING A BIRTHRIGHT

Only one event in Esau's earlier life is recorded in the Bible, but it is important as an indicator of Esau's character. Esau is described as "a cunning hunter." (Genesis 25:27.) Coming in from the field one day, Esau asked Jacob for "that same red pottage; for I am faint." "Sell me this day thy birthright," Jacob replied. Esau's answer is revealing: "*What profit shall this birthright do to me? . . .* And he sold his birthright unto Jacob." Moses, who wrote the book of Genesis, concludes the matter with this personal observation: "Thus Esau despised his birthright." (Genesis 25:30–34.)

A further testimony to Esau's disregard for the sacred blessings and promises of his heritage is related later when he chose his wives: "Esau was forty years old when he took to wife Judith the daughter of Beeri the Hittite, and Bashemath the daughter of Elon the Hittite: Which were a grief of mind unto Isaac and to Rebekah." (Genesis 26:34–35.)

The sacred blessings of the Abrahamic covenant with its attendant responsibilities could not be passed on through the unbelieving Canaanites. Esau's decisions indicate that at this juncture of his life, he placed little value upon the deepest desires of his parents' hearts. His immediate needs and desires controlled his actions without much thought of later consequences or blessings. This is a common trait of youth.

There is wisdom in frequently sitting down and pondering our own birthright as members of the Lord's Church and as children of an eternal Father in Heaven. We have the great truths of the scriptures and the gospel to live by. We may listen to the counsels of living prophets and apostles. We have the assurances of eternal family relationships through the sealing powers of the temple and the priesthood. We may be guided by the wonderful gift of the Holy Ghost. We can learn from the rich legacy of the past, complete with its many sacrifices. Perhaps our greatest birthright promise is the possibility, if we take advantage of all these aspects of our birthright, of becoming like our Savior and our Father in Heaven.

Sadly, like Esau, some members of the Church do not place high value on these tremendous blessings, and they make decisions that jeopardize the promises that accompany them. If they are not careful, without even realizing it, they may "sell" this precious birthright for more immediate and temporal concerns. In time, this leads to the shedding of Esau's tears.

"BLESS ME, EVEN ME ALSO"

Time passed in the life of Esau, and his father, Isaac, became blind as old age advanced. Desiring to bless his children before he died, he instructed Esau to bring him the savory meat that he loved. It was at this point that Rebekah convinced Jacob to take Esau's place and receive the birthright blessing. There has been much discussion about the honesty of Rebekah's and Jacob's actions, but if we focus on this, we will miss the message of Genesis. We must focus on the words of Esau, for the power and lesson of this part of the Old Testament is contained in his pleading voice.

When he returned and discovered that he had lost the blessing and that Isaac would confirm it upon his brother's head, "he cried with a great and exceeding bitter cry, and said unto his father, Bless me, even me also, O my father. . . . Hast thou not reserved a blessing for me?" Isaac replied with great emotion and love, "What shall I do *now* unto thee, my son?" The scriptures continue: "And Esau said unto his father, Hast thou but one blessing, my father? bless me, even me also, O my father. And Esau lifted up his voice, and wept." (Genesis 27:34–38.) When we place little value on the birthright in earlier years, we may fail to receive the desired blessings later in life.

While serving in various priesthood callings, I saw many people shed Esau's tears. Some of the most painful were shed by sisters of the ward or stake who, earlier in their lives, did not value greatly enough a temple marriage. They married a non-member or a less-active man. Years later, as their families began to grow, the assurances and promises of the gospel became more important to them. They wanted the blessings of full activity in the Church. This desire was often heightened as they watched other sisters in the ward attend the temple with their husbands and their sons advance in the priesthood and fill missions. Occasionally some of these situations worked out well, but most involved many anguished moments.

I have painful memories of these sisters entering the office and crying "with a great and exceeding bitter cry," "Bless me, bishop, even me also. Help me win my husband to full activity in the Church. Have you not reserved a blessing for me?" With other Church leaders, I would do all I could in such situations, but in spite of all our efforts, often the desired results were not obtained. Though I never said the words, I frequently reflected upon Isaac's question to his son, "What shall I do *now* unto thee?"

Sometimes Esau's tears were shed by parents. I recall the tears of a father who deeply wanted his son to fill a mission and marry in the temple. When his son was a boy, this father took him to sporting events on Sunday. The father played in a sports league in his community, and usually the games and tournaments extended into the Sabbath. He justified the many meetings he missed by saying, "I'm spending time with my son."

A later crisis in the life of this father changed his whole perspective on life. He became deeply committed to the gospel and one of the most active members of the ward. Unfortunately, his son did not share his enthusiasm. He was now playing the sport his father had taught him. He wanted to continue the old patterns and resented his father's change.

I watched that father break into a "bitter cry" one Sunday afternoon. "Bless me, even me also. Hast thou not reserved a blessing for me?" We did all we could, but the lure of the playing field was greater than the call of the mission field. Once again I sadly pondered Isaac's question: "What shall I do *now* unto thee, my son?"

Paul, commenting later on Esau's life, said, "Afterward, when he would have inherited the blessing, he was rejected: for he found no place of repentance, though he sought it carefully with tears." (Hebrews 12:17.) Paul is not saying there is no hope or repentance for Esau, but he lost certain blessings that even tears and sorrow could not bring back. If we put the two

major stories of Esau's life together, they teach this powerful lesson: *If we despise our birthrights, if we ask what profit they will
bring us and sell them cheaply, we will not receive the blessings.* If
we accept this truth, believe it, and act upon it, we will clear a
mist spread by the tempter.

"GREAT CHARACTERS IN HISTORY"

Joseph F. Smith taught, "Great characters in history were
selected early in life; and the best men in all ages gave their
young manhood to the service of God who honored them
abundantly with commendation and approval. . . . You may
look around today, and who are the leaders among the people
but those who early and zealously devoted themselves to the
faith? And you may foretell who are to be the leaders by observ-
ing the boys who show self-respect and purity and who are
earnest in all good works. . . . The opposite course, waiting to
serve the Lord until the wild oats of youth are sown, is repre-
hensible. There is always something lacking in the man who
spends his youth in wickedness and sin, and then turns to righteousness in later years. Of course, the Lord honors his repentance, and it is better far that a man should late turn from evil
than to continue in sin all his days, but the fact is clear that the
best part of his life and strength is wasted, and there remains
only poor, broken service to offer the Lord. There are regrets
and heart burnings in repenting late in life from the follies and
sins of youth, but there are consolation and rich reward in serving the Lord in the vigorous days of early manhood." (*Gospel
Doctrine*, 5th ed. [Salt Lake City: Deseret Book Co., 1939],
pp. 334–35.)

Esau's life would truly be tragic if it ended with his bitter cry.
Fortunately, his story does not end with tears but with hope.
Esau did avoid the mist Satan sends to those, like Esau, who
have sold their birthrights or sinned deeply. It is a mist
designed, like that in Lehi's dream, to obscure our Father in

Heaven's forgiving love, a mist Lucifer hopes will fill our hearts with despair.

SONS OR SERVANTS?

It did not take Esau long to realize why he had lost the blessing. Jacob had not really stolen it; rather, he had earned it. Esau took immediate steps to change his life. His change began when he witnessed his father bless Jacob again.

"When Esau saw that Isaac had blessed Jacob, and sent him away to Padan-aram, to take him a wife from thence; and that as he blessed him he gave him a charge, saying, Thou shalt not take a wife of the daughters of Canaan; and that Jacob obeyed his father and his mother, and was gone to Padan-aram; and Esau seeing that the daughters of Canaan pleased not Isaac his father; then went Esau unto Ishmael, and took unto the wives which he had Mahalath the daughter of Ishmael Abraham's son." (Genesis 28:6–9.)

Years later, when Jacob returned with his family, Esau had forgotten the past, and a beautiful scene of reconciliation and forgiveness ensued: "Esau ran to meet him, and embraced him, and fell on his neck, and kissed him: and they wept." (Genesis 33:4.)

Fully recognizing the birthright position of his brother Jacob, Esau willingly left the land, allowing his father's blessing to fall to Jacob unopposed: "And Esau took his wives, and his sons, and his daughters, and all the persons of his house, and his cattle, and all his beasts, and all his substance, which he had got in the land of Canaan; and went into the country from the face of his brother Jacob." (Genesis 36:6.) Esau had learned from life, and in the eternities, I feel confident, he will receive a full reward. The beautiful description of Esau's meeting with his brother uses almost exactly the same words as those used by Jesus in the parable of the Prodigal Son. It is to that parable we now turn to answer a question all returning prodigals ask: When I come home, do I come as a servant or as a son?

"NO MORE WORTHY TO BE CALLED THY SON"

I have a friend who made Esau decisions earlier in his life. In spite of many conversations and examinations of the scriptures, he has not yet forgiven himself for his past transgressions. He has not yet allowed the Savior the full victory He won for us all in Gethsemane. He has been active in the Church now for over thirty years, but he still feels like a lesser member of the kingdom. There yet remains in his mind the last thin remnants of a mist designed to veil the Father's love and the Savior's victory.

Of all the stories Jesus told, I love that of the Prodigal Son the most. It took me years of teaching it to fully understand the central question it asks us to ponder. The answer to that question is necessary to clear the mist that still troubles my friend. When the prodigal son returned home, was he a son or a servant?

The younger son had demanded his inheritance, left his home, and then "wasted his substance with riotous living. And when he had spent all, there arose a mighty famine in that land; and he began to be in want. . . . And when he came to himself, he said, How many hired servants of my father's have bread enough and to spare, and I perish with hunger!" (Luke 15:13–17.) For the longest time, I believed it was his destitute situation that brought the prodigal home. This contributed to his decision, without question, but something else turned his footsteps homeward—the memory of his father.

"I will arise and go to my father, and will say unto him, Father, I have sinned against heaven, and before thee, and am no more worthy to be called thy son: make me as one of thy hired servants." (Luke 15:18–19.) Often when people have wasted their substance, squandered an inheritance, or sold a birthright and then come to themselves, desiring to return home, they return feeling like the prodigal. "I realize I cannot return on the same standing as before," they think. "I am no longer a son or daughter and will be content to be a servant as long as I can come home."

When the boy returned home, was he greeted as a servant or as a son? "And he arose, and came to his father. But when he was yet a great way off, his father saw him, and had compassion, and ran, and fell on his neck and kissed him." (Luke 15:20.) It is important that we read the next verse with the right tone. If we read the prodigal son's words in a tone of amazement, we will more fully understand the power of the Savior's story.

"And the son said unto him, Father, I have sinned against heaven, and in thy sight, and am no more worthy to be called thy son." (Luke 15:21.) Here we might add, "Why are you treating me as one?" Notice that he left off the last part of his confession. He did not say, "Make me as one of thy hired servants." He had been greeted as a son. To make sure that the boy had no doubt of his father's forgiveness and also of his acceptance back into the family as a son, "the father said to his servants, Bring forth the best robe, and put it on him; and put a ring on his hand, and shoes on his feet; and bring hither the fatted calf, and kill it; and let us eat, and be merry: For this my son was dead, and is alive again; he was lost, and is found." (Luke 15:22–24.)

A REAL PRODIGAL SON—ALMA

Satan would have us believe that we cannot return as sons and daughters. This mist is also employed to blind the eyes of the elder sons and daughters of the kingdom who may not be willing to receive the returning prodigals as openly as the father. Lest we have any doubt about the full acceptance of prodigals into the kingdom and their possibility of a full inheritance, again we need only read the story of Alma the Younger in the

Book of Mormon. Alma played out the story of the prodigal son in reality. He also mentioned his own unworthiness and was amazed at the extent of God's mercy. Not only was he accepted back into the kingdom, but he also rose to leadership within it.

This sounds somewhat contradictory to the lessons discussed in the last chapter, especially in light of what President Joseph F. Smith said. However, the scriptures always present the proper balance of warning and encouragement, of justice and mercy, of comfort and exhortation. Each story must be applied in the way the Holy Spirit instructs us to apply it. No principle of the gospel will be true to itself if applied in the same manner all the time. Lucifer's mists are often designed to apply a correct principle at the wrong time: to focus on mercy when the mind should be pondering the justice of God, or to focus on despair at the Lord's exhortations and warnings when His compassion and comforting words should dominate our thoughts.

"I WILL NOURISH YOU"

The scriptures include a second witness to the assurance that we can return as sons and daughters and not as servants. That witness is found in the story that is most associated with loving forgiveness, that of Joseph and his brothers. In this story the question we are invited to answer is a bit different, but the truth to which it testifies is the same. When we repent, are we servants, or are we brothers and sisters?

Joseph had not seen his brothers for over twenty years when they came to Egypt seeking food. Seeing their anguish and guilt over their selling of him, Joseph wept, embraced them, and forgave them. Their families, including Jacob, were brought into Egypt, and Jacob lived in Egypt for seventeen years. (See Genesis 47:28.) At his death, the brothers feared that Joseph would hate them and seek revenge for their earlier treachery. "And they sent a message unto Joseph saying, Thy father did command before he died, saying, So shall ye say unto Joseph,

Forgive, I pray thee now, the trespass of thy brethren, and their sin; for they did unto thee evil: and now, we pray thee, forgive the trespass of the servants of the God of thy father." (Genesis 50:16–17.)

Joseph wept when he heard these words. He wept over the fact that his brothers had still not forgiven themselves and felt anguish and fear over their past transgressions, even though their sin was almost forty years in the past. "And his brethren also went and fell down before his face; and they said, *Behold, we be thy servants.*" (Genesis 50:18.) Like the prodigal son, the brothers did not expect to be treated like brothers; they were content to be servants. In their own minds that was all they were worthy to be. But "Joseph said unto them, Fear not: for am I in the place of God? But as for you, ye thought evil against me; but God meant it unto good, to bring to pass, as it is this day, to save much people alive. Now therefore *fear ye not: I will nourish you, and your little ones.* And he *comforted them, and spake kindly unto them.*" (Genesis 50:19–21.)

The story of Joseph testifies to us that when we seek forgiveness, when we recognize our past mistakes, we will receive comfort and kind words. We will be accepted as full brothers and sisters back into the family, not as servants unworthy of a former relationship we have lost.

"NONE OF IT MATTERS NOW"

I believe the most tender and touching scene I have ever witnessed took place between a wife and husband. Many years earlier the husband had committed adultery. When he "came to himself," he sought forgiveness from his wife. She freely gave it, and they worked on their marriage earnestly. More than twenty-five years had passed. Occasionally the husband would remember, and the sorrow, pain, and guilt would return. A situation with one of their children brought the painful memories back to the husband. He sat in my office with his wife and began to weep, blaming all their present trials upon his past actions. His wife rose from her chair, walked to his side, put her arms around him, and kissed his forehead and temples. She wiped his tears, smoothed his hair, and said over and over again, "It was a long time ago, and none of it matters now."

She had long ago cleared a dangerous mist that could have blocked her own vision and was doing all she could to clear it for him also. There are no servants in the Church, only sons and daughters, brothers and sisters.

CHAPTER TWENTY-FIVE

SEEING WITH ZENIFF'S EYES

The Savior often describes the latter days as a time filled with "wars, and rumors of wars." (Joseph Smith—Matthew 1:23, 28.) Today we would use the word *threats* instead of *rumors*. It is evident from what we hear almost constantly in the news that we do live in a time when nations are either engaged in war or live under the threat of one. The greatest example of a "rumor" of a war in the last century was the Cold War.

On a smaller scale, racial and religious problems within communities trouble their peace, and family breakups threaten the very foundation of society. Whether on the larger scale of nations or the more intimate one of interpersonal relationships, one type of mist seems to be behind it all. In the Book of Mormon, Zeniff saw through that mist, and with his vision we find a powerful solution to counter the tragic consequences seen far too often on the nightly news.

WRONGED AND WROTH

Before leading his people into battle against the Lamanites, Zeniff explained to them why they were being attacked: "They were a wild, and ferocious, and a blood-thirsty people, believing in the tradition of their fathers, which is this—Believing that they were . . . *wronged* in the wilderness by their brethren, and they were also *wronged* while crossing the sea; and again, that they were *wronged* while in the land of their first inheritance." (Mosiah 10:12–13.) The key word in this passage is clearly *wronged.*

What is the normal response when people feel they have been wronged? Zeniff's account reveals the answer: "[Nephi's] brethren were *wroth* with him because they understood not the dealings of the Lord; they were also *wroth* with him upon the waters. . . . And again, they were *wroth* with him when they had arrived in the promised land. . . . And again, they were *wroth* with him because he departed into the wilderness." (Mosiah 10:14–16.) When a wrong, real or perceived, has been inflicted, the natural response is be angry.

The combination of "wronged" and "wroth" leads to hatred. Zeniff concluded his explanation with this result: "And thus they have taught their children that they should hate them, and that they should murder them, and that they should rob and plunder them, and do all they could to destroy them; therefore they have *an eternal hatred* towards the children of Nephi." (Mosiah 10:17.)

We also read of hatred in an earlier description of the Nephite and Lamanite troubles. Enos noted the Nephite efforts "to restore the Lamanites unto the true faith in God." However, their "labors were vain; their *hatred was fixed.*" (Enos 1:20.)

A close examination of various areas in the world today reveals this all-too-familiar pattern. In the Middle East the Palestinians, and to an extent the Israelis also, feel they have been wronged. We have all seen graphic images of the anger and hatred these real and perceived wrongs have created. In the Balkans, similar wrongs, anger, and hatred have resulted in the massacre of whole villages and in long lines of refugees pouring into neighboring countries. Problems in central Africa and religious differences in India and Ireland reveal similar patterns.

Racial tensions in America are traced to past wrongs, with anger and hatred passed down through generations. Within families, divorce often follows an accumulation of wrongs between husband and wife. Anger and frustration follow, and love is replaced with bitterness and hatred.

THE BLINDING SMOKE OF HELL

The blinding power of this type of mist is powerfully described in the book of Revelation, using symbolic language. John "saw a star fall from heaven unto the earth; and to him was given the key of the bottomless pit." The fallen star is an obvious reference to Lucifer, who was cast out of heaven. With his key in hand, Lucifer "opened the bottomless pit; and there arose a smoke out of the pit, as the smoke of a great furnace. . . . And there came out of the smoke locusts upon the earth." (Revelation 9:1–3.) The locusts spread out over the earth to destroy people as thoroughly as a real plague of locusts destroys green plants. These locusts represent the destructive forces of war; and the smoke of hatred, anger, and prejudice give them birth. Just as the smoke of a furnace would sting and blind the eyes of one opening its door, so does the smoke of hatred enrage people and blind them to the one thing they must see if there is any hope of ending the conflicts, whether national or familial.

Hatred and anger are such dangerous mists because they allow those seeking power over others to obtain that power. This is clearly demonstrated in the first of the war chapters at the end of the book of Alma. Amalickiah, seeking power over the Nephites, used hatred and anger to first obtain it over the Lamanites. "Now this he did that he *might preserve their hatred* towards the Nephites, that he might bring [the Lamanites] into subjection to the accomplishment of his designs. For behold, his designs were to *stir up the Lamanites to anger* against the Nephites; this he did *that he might usurp great power over them,* and also that he might gain power over the Nephites." (Alma 43:7–8.)

We have seen this type of control "usurped" over people by the great dictators of the past century, such as Adolf Hitler and Josef Stalin. People with hatred in their souls and anger in their hearts are easy to manipulate. From such beginnings great wars have been started, fought, and prolonged.

LEARNING TO SEE THE GOOD

That brings us back to Zeniff and his solution to "eternal, fixed hatred." Whenever the scriptures describe a problem, especially a widespread problem such as this one, we should look for counsel about that problem somewhere nearby in the text. We are introduced to Zeniff as a spy who had been sent "among the Lamanites that . . . [the Nephite] army might come upon them and destroy them." (Mosiah 9:1.) Zeniff originally came to the Lamanites with the standard mistrust and anger the Nephites had also built up over the years.

But something wonderful happened as he went about his spying business. "When I *saw that which was good among them* I was desirous that they should not be destroyed. . . . I would that our ruler should make a treaty with them." Later he approached the Lamanite king, desiring to "possess the land in *peace.*" (Mosiah 9:1, 2, 5.) When we learn to see the good in other races, nations, peoples, or members of our own family, treaties can be formulated and compromises established, and we can live in peace.

Earlier Jacob had encouraged his people to see the good in the Lamanites. The Nephites were filled with anger and hatred, judging the Lamanites to be inferior. They saw the "filthiness" of the Lamanites and the "darkness of their skins," but Jacob encouraged his people to focus on another aspect of Lamanite culture: "Behold, their husbands love their wives, and their wives love their husbands; and their husbands and their wives love their children." (Jacob 3:7.)

When I first went to the Middle East, I carried with me a rather grim view of the Palestinians. But once there, I found them to be generous, hospitable, warm, and kind. They are easy to love, in spite of the image that is sometimes portrayed in the news.

In counseling situations, how often have bishops heard couples arguing with each other, threatening to end their marriages, focusing always on the faults of their companion. If, however, each will look for the good in the other person, the anger, bitterness, and even hatred can begin to diminish. We can write it down as a rule that Satan delights when we focus on the wrongs we have received, or on the faults of others. In time, he can blind people so thoroughly with this mist, this smoke of hell, that even good qualities are changed to blackness and evil.

BROTHER AGAINST BROTHER

Often the problem of eternal hatred is compounded. Not all of the Nephites who were spying with Zeniff agreed with his assessment of the Lamanites. "I contended with my brethren in the wilderness," he wrote, "but [our ruler] being an austere and a blood-thirty man commanded that I should be slain; but I was rescued by the shedding of much blood; for father fought against father, and brother against brother." (Mosiah 9:2.) Far too frequently when some in one of the opposing parties see the good and desire peace, there are others so full of hate, anger, and mistrust that the suggestion of peace is looked upon as an act of treason. The conflict widened from Nephite against Lamanite to include Nephite against Nephite.

Egyptian leader Anwar Sadat was assassinated by some of his own people after he made peace with Israel. Likewise, Itzak

Rabin was assassinated by a Jewish settler for his attempts at peace with the Palestinians. When these kinds of complications arise, they may threaten the hope of peace and the end of hatred.

"THEY LAUGHED US TO SCORN"

Some may argue that Zeniff was wrong in his assessment of the Lamanites. He did make his treaty, but he related later that the seeming kindness and willingness for peace of the Lamanite king was merely a trap: "It was the cunning and the craftiness of king Laman, to bring my people into bondage, that he yielded up the land that we might possess it." (Mosiah 9:10.) Perhaps Zeniff's "austere and blood-thirsty" ruler had been right. The only way to deal with the Lamanites was to kill them before they killed the Nephites. Zeniff's great experiment in peace ended up in bondage and war. Eventually the remnants of the Nephites had to return to Zarahemla. Lest we come to this conclusion, the Book of Mormon relates another story that vindicates Zeniff's idealism.

The four sons of Mosiah were also accused of unrealistic idealism. In Ammon's homecoming report of the fourteen-year mission, he reminded his fellow laborers of the mockery they had endured before their departure: "They laughed us to scorn. For they said unto us: Do ye suppose that ye can bring the Lamanites to the knowledge of the truth? Do ye suppose that ye can convince the Lamanites of the incorrectness of the traditions of their fathers, as stiff-necked a people as they are, whose hearts delight in the shedding of blood; whose days have been spent in the grossest of iniquity; whose ways have been the ways of a transgressor from the beginning?" (Alma 26:23–24.)

In this passage the Nephites are so focused on the evil of their enemies that they can't see any good. Hence their suggestion to the four sons of Mosiah: "Moreover they did say:

Let us take up arms against them, that we destroy them and their iniquity out of the land, lest they overrun us and destroy us." (Alma 26:25.)

The four sons of Mosiah did more than Zeniff. Not only did they see the possibilities for good in the Lamanites, but they also believed they could be turned to the truth and give up centuries of hatred and tradition. Their idealism was richly rewarded as thousands accepted their testimonies, gave up their hatred, and buried their weapons of war. I cannot help but believe that one of the main reasons this story is included in the scriptures is to give hope in the gospel to a troubled and fractional world.

In families that are torn and bitter, often we hear one or both sides say, "He will never change!" Somehow this is supposed to justify the continued anger and bitterness. If the Lamanites, however, could change centuries of tradition and completely reverse their faith, values, and behavior, surely there is hope for every situation, whether international, national, or individual.

GREAT LOVE—GREAT JOY

In the midst of Ammon's missionary efforts, he was confronted by Lamoni's father, a man filled with anger and hatred of the Nephites. He was convinced that the missionaries could not be trusted and must therefore be destroyed. Ammon, however, shows us one of the great tools we may wield as we try to overcome this mist of the adversary. When he met the old king on the way to the land of Middoni with Lamoni to free his brothers, he was forced to fight with him. When Ammon prevailed, the king offered him half his kingdom in exchange for his life. Ammon asked only that his brothers be freed and that the king not be angry with his son.

"When he saw that Ammon *had no desire to destroy him,* and when he also saw *the great love he had for his son* Lamoni, he was astonished exceedingly." (Alma 20:26.) If one race or one people, or even a few individuals among them, can show the other side they truly have no desire to destroy them—if they can show them sincere love—the mists will begin to dissipate. These qualities as portrayed by Ammon changed the king's hatred, anger, and mistrust to an eagerness to learn. "I have been somewhat troubled in mind," he told Aaron when he came to teach him, "because of the *generosity and the greatness* of the words of thy brother Ammon." (Alma 22:3.)

Unfortunately, just as we saw earlier with the fighting between Zeniff and his ruler, the unconverted Lamanites viewed their converted brothers as traitors and attacked them. In time, this complexity of hatred drove the Anti-Nephi-Lehis out of the land. Once again, in spite of partial, even spectacular success, hatred won out in the end as the converted Lamanites were forced out of their land into the lands of the Nephites. It is not easy to conquer the thick mist of hatred, but every effort to penetrate it, as through the vision of Zeniff and that of the four sons of Mosiah, must be applied. We must believe that seeing goodness and showing love will ultimately triumph. The resulting joy, even in limited success, as Ammon and his brothers would testify, is worth all the suffering it may take to accomplish it: "We have suffered all manner of afflictions, and all this, that perhaps we might be the means of saving some soul; and we supposed that our joy would be full if perhaps we could be the means of saving some. Now behold, we can look forth and see the fruits of our labors; and are they few? I say unto you, Nay, they are many; yea, and we can witness of their sincerity, because of their love towards their brethren and also towards us." (Alma 26:30–31.)

Few of us will be placed in a situation where we can overcome major international conflicts. However, in our own minds we can constantly search for the good in all people and nations. Perhaps, more important, we can learn to focus on the good in our neighbors, in fellow Saints, and especially in our families.

When all the world sees with Zeniff's eyes, mankind will begin to understand the heart of deity, for God himself views all His children in this manner. May we see as we are seen.

CHAPTER TWENTY-SIX

BEATING DOWN
THE GOPHER

I have been fascinated with the
language and the images John uses in the book of Revelation.
His symbol for the tempter is a red dragon with seven heads.
When dealing with figurative writing, it is necessary to stop
often and try to discern what the symbol is teaching or suggesting to the mind. I have wondered why John gave the dragon
seven heads. Why not just one? I believe there are multiple
reasons for the many heads. Perhaps the most practical reason
is to prepare us to better fight him. The most dangerous and
foolish thing one could do while fighting a seven-headed
dragon would be to focus on a single head while ignoring the
others. Satan has many faces. One of the major purposes of this
work has been to reveal some of those faces as they are
described in the scriptures. Each of us may confront more or
less danger from various heads. It is wise to be aware of them
all, but I believe that one of the heads is a favorite of the adversary, and we must all learn to avoid it. It is the head of pride—
particularly the pride that arises from wealth and the desire for
material things.

I have been struck on more than one occasion by how many

of Lucifer's statements deal with money and the treasures of mortality. I have also been struck by how little that is positive the scriptures have to say about riches. There are literally dozens of warnings about wealth in the scriptures but little that is favorable. We need to keep a sharp lookout for all of the dragon's heads, but this one we must be keenly aware of, for it strikes with such subtlety.

There are many deceptions this mist of materialism hides. I've found five major ones to be particularly harmful. I've tried to clear them by frequently reminding myself of the following phrases and the principles they represent: "You can't catch a snipe." "Wooed by the right woman." "Never close the back door." "Win the marathon, not the hundred-yard dash." "Beat down the gopher."

"YOU CAN'T CATCH A SNIPE"

The first deception simply asserts that happiness comes with possessions. One of the reasons Laman and Lemuel murmured so constantly was their acceptance of this claim. "Behold," they said, "these many years we have suffered in the wilderness, which time we might have *enjoyed our possessions* and the land of our inheritance; yea, and *we might have been happy.*" (1 Nephi 17:21.) The Lord sent the boys back twice to Jerusalem, but not for possessions. Rather, they went back for the two things the Lord wants us to understand are most precious—the truths of the scriptures and family.

In contrast to Laman and Lemuel's belief, Lehi clearly taught, "If there be no righteousness there be no *happiness.*" (2 Nephi 2:13.) Righteousness is equal to happiness! Remember, in the dream, Laman and Lemuel did not come to the "tree, whose fruit was desirable to make one *happy.*" (1 Nephi 8:10.) We are not told where the brothers ended up in the dream, but we can be fairly confident that they were attracted to the spacious building, where everyone's "manner of dress was exceedingly fine." (1 Nephi 8:27.)

When I was about ten years old, I was fooled quite conclusively on an evening snipe hunt. My uncle had learned how to take somebody in—hook, line, and sinker. "There will be a snipe moon tonight," he said casually. "Maybe we can catch some." A snipe moon was a little sliver of moon with no light. When I asked what a snipe was, he replied, "A snipe is a little bird that can't fly. They are brown and run on little trails all through the sagebrush. They are stupid, and if you hold a gunny sack on the trail with the mouth open, they will run right in. If you make a clucking sound deep in your throat, it draws them to you."

I was supposed to practice the call during the day until I got it right. As the evening darkened, all the boys gathered in a knot to watch the fun. Their job was to circle through the sagebrush and drive the imaginary birds toward me. My uncle then said, "I haven't caught a snipe in a few years. Do you mind if I come along and sit next to you? We can watch both directions of the trail."

He then ran down to the barn alone to get a gunny sack. He also stopped at the hen house, picked out a fat hen, stuffed her into his coat, zipped it up, and held her still. Since it was dark, I could not see the bulge in his coat.

Arriving on the hill, he began clucking for snipes. In a few minutes he said, "I hear them coming." He unzipped his coat, grasped the hen by the legs, and then stood up and swung her around his head, yelling, "I've got mine!" Turning to look, I saw a large bird flapping in the darkness, just before he plunged her deep into the bottom of his sack. He then held the sack up in front of him so I could see it dancing and swinging with the motion of the hen.

"You can have all the rest!" he said as he left with his prize. After that demonstration, I stayed on the hillside for hours hoping for similar success. Finally I gave up and was met with hoots of laughter from the others. "You can't catch a snipe!" echoed in my head. "There ain't no such bird!"

"THE GRANDEST SNIPE HUNT OF ALL"

The belief that possessions and riches can bring happiness is the grandest snipe hunt of all. As mentioned in an earlier chapter, this belief often leads to making bricks without straw. We labor constantly to obtain more in the hope that the snipe of happiness and fulfillment will suddenly fly into our open bag. The sad thing is, many people never come down off the hill. They remain in the sagebrush, clutching their open sack and perpetually clucking to something that isn't there.

The book of Helaman describes the Nephites when they were deeply caught in the mist of materialism. "Ye ought to marvel because ye are given away that the devil has got so great hold upon your hearts," Nephi warned. He then continued by telling them the means by which that hold had been obtained: "Ye have set your hearts upon the riches and the vain things of this world." (Helaman 7:15, 21.)

From the walls of Zarahemla, Samuel the Lamanite provided a second witness to Nephi. "Your riches [are] cursed because ye have set your hearts upon them," he warned. "Ye do always remember your riches." (Helaman 13:21–22.) Samuel then assured them they would one day realize it had all been a snipe hunt: "Ye have sought all the days of your lives for that which *ye could not obtain;* and ye have sought for happiness in doing iniquity, which thing is contrary to the nature of that righteousness which is in our great and Eternal Head." (Helaman 13:38.)

If we feel ourselves getting too caught up in a desire for more and more things, believing that the next possession will surely bring the anticipated happiness, it is helpful to remember, "You can't catch a snipe. There ain't no such bird!"

"WOOED BY THE RIGHT WOMAN"

The above deception is particularly effective because possessions do give a certain temporary joy. This is where the second mist is deployed. When the pleasure of one thing begins to fade and we haven't yet learned that lasting happiness is not in wealth or worldly things, there is forever a new possession to desire and acquire. Isaiah, Ezekiel, and John the Beloved all tell us the same thing. There is always something to buy in Babylon. Ezekiel and John give long lists of the luxury goods that were up for sale in their own world that everyone just had to have. (See Ezekiel 27 and Revelation 18.)

Babylon (or sometimes the ancient trading city of Tyre) is the symbol these prophets use to describe the materialistic world. Babylon is portrayed in scripture as a beautiful woman who is very much aware of her power over others. She wants their gifts and woos her admirers perpetually. "Thine heart was lifted up because of thy beauty, thou hast corrupted thy wisdom by reason of thy brightness." (Ezekiel 28:17.) "Thou saidst, I shall be a lady for ever." (Isaiah 47:7.)

Knowing her attractiveness, she entices all to come to her, to build her up, to spend their wealth in her bazaars. "Bring your time, your talents, your labors, your resources to me," she cries. It is not so much that her wares are evil; there is just no end to the multiplicity of what she has to offer. John's long list of what you can buy in Babylon ends with the words "and souls of men." (Revelation 18:13.) You can buy anything in the world if you have enough money. That is all that matters, and she will make sure there is never an end to what she offers, for she knows she can give only transitory fulfillment. Her only hope of maintaining our devotion is to continue to offer new dainty, delicious delicacies. (See Revelation 18:3, 7, 14.) When the thrill of the old possessions begins to wane, some new thing will be offered to replace them.

Zion is also described in scripture as a beautiful woman. She also invites us to come to her, to build her up. "Bring your time, your talents, your labors, your resources to me," she calls. "Babylon will eventually fall, but I will increase in beauty. The only real lasting happiness is found in me." Almost daily we listen to the voices of these two women. There is a tendency to think we can keep both of them happy, but in time the choice must be made. With which woman will our heart lie? "Ye cannot serve God and mammon," Jesus warned. (Matthew 6:24.) In times of plenty, Babylon cries, "You can always buy more!" During these same times, Zion teaches, "Use the good times to eliminate debt! Use the days of plenty to prepare for the future, not to continually consume."

It is true that the goods of the world are not evil. The Lord wants us to have what we need "in abundance." (D&C 49:19.) As we listen to the voices of those who would woo us to their side, we must actively seek the direction of the Spirit. Only in this can we hope to find the proper balance between what is sufficient for our needs and what is merely the satisfaction of our desires. This becomes increasingly easier when we realize that nothing we own really belongs to us.

"NEVER CLOSE THE BACK DOOR"

Jesus told a parable about a man who prospered and planned on doing a lot of shopping in Babylon. He prefaced this parable by saying, "Take heed, and beware of covetousness: for a man's life consisteth not in the abundance of the things which he possesseth." (Luke 12:15.) If we are not careful, we may become wealthy in goods but impoverished in living. While reflecting on purchasing a house, Henry David Thoreau wrote, "The cost of a thing is the amount of what I will call life which is required to be exchanged for it, immediately or in the long run." (*Walden and Other Writings* [New York: Random House, 1950], pp. 27–28.)

The Savior spoke of a rich man whose ground had "brought

forth plentifully: And he thought within himself, saying, What shall I do, because I have no room where to bestow my fruits? And he said, This will I do: I will pull down my barns, and build greater; and there will I bestow all my fruits and my goods. And I will say to my soul, Soul, thou hast much goods laid up for many years; take thine ease, eat, drink, and be merry." (Luke 12:16–19.)

Notice how many times the words *I* and *my* are used in the rich man's statements. But were his riches really his? We shall see. Like Laman and Lemuel, this man was sure that happiness was found in the enjoyment of many goods. He also gave in to the human tendency to always want to "build greater." And why shouldn't we have finer and finer things, we argue? We have worked hard. Our resources belong to us. Have we not earned bigger houses, fancier automobiles, faster boats, and the latest technological wonders?

"But God said unto him, Thou fool, this night thy soul shall be required of thee: *then whose shall those things be, which thou hast provided?* So is he that layeth up treasure for himself, and is not rich toward God." (Luke 12:20–21.) For the longest time I answered the Lord's question as follows: "The goods will belong to his children or those still living." In time I learned that the proper answer is, "They have always belonged to the Lord and will remain in His hands."

When we fully acknowledge this truth, which is the foundational principle of the law of consecration, we will have taken the biggest step we can toward clearing the mist of materialism. Then when we hear the wooing voice of Babylon parading her delicacies before us, we can answer, "Your goods look wonderful, but I must spend my labors and the rewards I receive for them the way their owner desires. If it were my money I would acquire your wares, but since all that I have belongs to the Lord, I must consult with Him first." When we begin to think in this way, we change the way we make financial decisions.

When we contemplate purchasing a house, a car, a recreational vehicle, a boat, stereo equipment, and so on, we ask the Lord if we can expend His resources, not our own, on these items. If we think in this way, in most cases we will decrease considerably our expenditures of time and resources.

This type of thinking brings benefits in a number of areas. For over ten years, when our children were smaller and were all living at home, we needed a van. Perhaps you have discovered, as my wife and I did, that when you own a van, it quickly becomes the ward's van. We were constantly hauling youth to camp, activities, and conferences. We used it to transport Relief Society decorations and food. We were putting thousands of miles a year on our van for the Church. For a while I was frustrated with this, until the Lord gently reminded me that it was not my van but His. I don't mind a bit putting miles on the Lord's van. When the Lord's van wears out, He'll see that there are means to replace it.

One way of looking at consecration is to compare it to a house with a front and back door. The Lord opens the front door and hands in His gifts. These may come in the form of opportunities, wealth, talents, and other resources. We take from these gifts sufficient for our needs. The Lord in his goodness, and to test us, often hands in more than we need. What do we do with the surplus? Babylon says, "Come shopping. Fill your house with all I have to offer. In time you may even need a bigger house to hold it all. Keep the back door closed."

We resist this voice, however, open the back door, and use the surplus according to the Lord's desires. We try to build up Zion, help the poor, support the spread of the gospel, redeem the dead, and so on. The Lord now opens the front door and passes in more things. "What will you do with this?" He asks us. Once again, according to our changing circumstances, we remove sufficient for our needs, open the back door, and dispense with the rest. This goes on for a lifetime, and the

temptation always exists to shut the back door and let the surplus accumulate while we, like the rich fool in the parable,
"Take [our] ease, eat, drink, and [are] merry."

"WIN THE MARATHON, NOT THE HUNDRED-YARD DASH"

Consecration poses a real problem for Lucifer's most effective mist. But he knows that, if he is patient, there is a real possibility that the back door may eventually be closed or at least
narrowed. Though it is possible to resist the power of wealth for
a time, continuing to do so throughout life is rare. We may win
the hundred-yard dash but fail to endure in the marathon.

Twice in the Book of Mormon we see this happen. The first
chapter of Alma describes the Nephite attitude toward wealth,
which is exactly what the Lord desires: "They did impart of
their substance, every man according to that which he had, to
the poor, and the needy, and the sick, and the afflicted; and
they did not wear costly apparel, yet they were neat and comely.
. . . And now, because of the steadiness of the church they
began to be exceedingly rich, having abundance of all things
whatsoever they stood in need. . . . And thus, in their prosper-
ous circumstances, they did not send away any who were
naked, or that were hungry, or that were athirst, or that were
sick, or that had not been nourished; and they did not set their
hearts upon riches; therefore they were liberal to all." (Alma
1:27, 29–30.) There are no mists here!

The year belonging to this wonderful description is given as
90 B.C. Let us take a peek at the same people just a few years
later. We read the following description for 84 B.C.: "The people
of the church began to wax proud, because of their exceeding
riches, and their fine silks, and their fine-twined linen, and
because of their many flocks and herds, and their gold and their
silver, and all manner of precious things, which they had
obtained by their industry; and in all these things were they

lifted up in the pride of their eyes, for they began to wear very costly apparel. . . . The people of the church began to set their hearts upon riches and upon the vain things of the world." (Alma 4:6, 8.)

One of the great fallacies of life is the belief that we can always do what we can do some of the time. Most of us can handle the hundred-yard dash temptations, but we also need to finish the marathons. In case we miss the message of the first chapters of Alma, we see a repeat performance in a later generation. After the Nephite wars, Mormon recorded, "They began to grow exceedingly rich. But notwithstanding their riches, or their strength, or their prosperity, they were not lifted up in the pride of their eyes; neither were they slow to remember the Lord their God; but they did humble themselves exceedingly before him." (Alma 62:48–49.) The date of this entry is 57 B.C.

A decade later pride began to grow, and within a few years "there was peace also, save it were the pride which began to enter into the church—not into the church of God, but into the hearts of the people who professed to belong to the church of God—And they were lifted up in pride. . . . And it was because of their exceedingly great riches and their prosperity in the land; and it *did grow upon them from day to day*." (Helaman 3:33–34, 36.)

One of the greatest difficulties of prosperity is resisting the pride that so naturally arises from it. Therefore, I try to remind myself continually to "beat down the gopher."

"BEAT DOWN THE GOPHER"

While teaching a class at BYU one semester, I conducted an interesting experiment with the class. We were studying the problem of wealth in the book of Jacob. Jacob told his people, "Because some of you have *obtained more abundantly* than that of your brethren ye are lifted up in the pride of your hearts, and wear stiff necks and high heads because of the costliness of your apparel, and persecute your brethren because *ye suppose that ye are better than they.*" (Jacob 2:13.)

Jacob hit the nail of pride right on the head. When we obtain more abundantly, there is a great temptation to think we are better than others. This is often reflected in outward things. I asked the students what they considered to be the equivalent of costly apparel in American society. They answered, "The house you live in and its neighborhood, and the car you drive." In their assessment, clothing, although still a symbol for pride, was not as demonstrative as a house and car.

Pride is so difficult to conquer because every difference between two people is an invitation for pride to enter. We decided to try an experiment. For one week we would carry three-by-five cards in our pockets and write down every time we were tempted to think "I am better" because of some per-ceived difference. At the end of the week we compared notes. We all learned that we had considerably more trouble with pride than we had thought.

For example, certain apartment complexes carried more prestige than others. This was also true of certain dorms on campus. The degrees being worked on were also compared. Engineering and law, for instance, were seen as better than ele-mentary education. The state you came from was important. California held more status than Idaho in some minds. For those coming from the Wasatch Front area, the high school they attended held weight. There were also the expected judg-ments based on clothing, physical beauty, weight, and cars.

As fate would have it, that very week I found out my uncle was moving to Palm Springs, and his "exclusive" clothing store was going out of business. He sent me a gift of a new overcoat that cost hundreds of dollars. It was beautiful. I put it on and walked across campus looking at all the less-exclusive over-coats. I had to laugh at myself for giving in so easily to the feelings of pride produced by this gift. I went home, hung the coat in the closet, and put on my old one. I'm not sure I have the strength to wear that expensive coat even today.

When I lived in California, we had a lot of problems with gophers in the backyard. My mother gave me the job of controlling them. I tried many different methods to get rid of them, for they made a mess of the lawn. I set traps, flooded their holes with the garden hose, and used bait. Sometimes I would sit quietly behind their dirt mounds waiting for them to surface and then try to beat them down with a baseball bat. "Maybe if they get clobbered every time they poke their heads up," I thought, "they will leave and dig their holes somewhere else." I never did completely succeed, but the lawn would have been a disaster if I had stopped trying.

Pride is like a gopher in the backyard of our souls. It has a hundred different holes, and it can pop up anywhere and at any time to suggest that we are somehow better than others. Our only recourse is to beat it down every time we see it.

This I tried to do all during the experiment week at BYU. I knocked every proud thought out of my head. At the end of the week, I noticed that they were coming less frequently. I stood there with my bat surveying the backyard of my soul, waiting for the gopher to peek out and try again. He stayed underground, and I found myself saying, "By golly, I've conquered pride. There aren't many people who can do that. I must be better than others." There, sitting on my bat, was the gopher, laughing at me for being proud of my humility.

Benjamin Franklin tried hard to control pride. After a long battle he wrote his assessment of his efforts: "In reality, there is, perhaps, no one of our natural passions so hard to subdue as pride. Disguise it, struggle with it, beat it down, stifle it, mortify it as much as one pleases, it is still alive, and will every now and then peep out and show itself; you will see it, perhaps, often in this history; for, even if I could conceive that I had completely

overcome it, I should probably be proud of my humility."
(*Autobiography of Benjamin Franklin* [London: Heron Books,
1904], p. 83.)

LAZARUS AND THE RICH MAN

To help his people clear the mist of pride, Jacob taught them
that "one being is as precious in [God's] sight as the other. And
all flesh is of the dust; and for the selfsame end hath he created
them." (Jacob 2:21.)

In a parable, the Savior described "a certain rich man, which
was clothed in purple and fine linen, and fared sumptuously
every day: and there was a certain beggar named Lazarus,
which was laid at his gate, full of sores." (Luke 16:19–20.)

Is it just a coincidence that Jesus gave the beggar a name and
not the rich man? In a worldly way of thinking, it is usually the
wealthy person who is well known, while the nameless masses
of the poor are just faces in the crowd. Notice now how the
Savior describes the deaths of both men: "And it came to pass,
that the beggar died, and was carried by the angels into
Abraham's bosom: the rich man also died, and was buried."
(Luke 16:22.) The eloquent description is reserved for the beggar. The death of the rich man is given almost as a postscript.
Once again, the irony is apparent. Usually we would describe
the death of the poor in such terse terms.

When the rich man, in the torments of hell, asks Abraham
to allow Lazarus to cool his thirst with a drop of water,
Abraham replies, "Between us and you there is a great gulf
fixed: so that they which would pass from hence to you cannot;
neither can they pass to us, that would come from thence."
(Luke 16:26.)

We must catch the irony in Abraham's words and not just
the doctrinal implications. In life we often place great gulfs
between people of different economic classes, races, and

educational levels. During some past times and today in many places the barriers that separate people are great.

As an outsider moving to Salt Lake City years ago, I soon discovered that I-15 created a kind of barrier between the west and the east sides of the city. Barriers are always an invitation to pride, whether they be economic, geographic, educational, or ethical. As Jacob warned his people, we must forever be on our guard by remembering that "one being is as precious in [God's] sight as the other."

GRATITUDE—PRIDE'S ENEMY

The combination of these five ideas has helped me to fight this head of the dragon—this mist of deception. I would add one more thought that is given by Moses. It is especially helpful for a people whom the Lord has abundantly blessed: "When thou hast eaten and art full, then thou shalt bless the Lord thy God for the good land which he hath given thee." (Deuteronomy 8:10.) One of the surest weapons I know of against pride is gratitude. Pride, covetousness, and materialism cannot exist in the heart at the same time as gratitude. Gratitude recognizes that all we have is a gift from God, which is the underlying assumption of consecration. If we fully and humbly thank the Lord for all we have received at His hand, a powerful mist will dissipate, and we may not need to remind ourselves so often that you can't catch a snipe and to beat down the gopher.

CHAPTER TWENTY-SEVEN

COME OUT OF
THE WORLD!

I have saved for this chapter what
I believe to be the greatest of all mist-clearing motivations. It
has to do with our feelings for the Savior. After all, the war in
heaven was basically fought over whom we wanted to follow as
our redeemer—Lucifer or Jehovah.

The scriptures often speak of offering the Savior a broken
heart. From the literal mists of darkness covering the Nephite
lands after the Crucifixion, the voice of the Savior was heard
asking the people to bring Him a gift: "Ye shall offer for a sacrifice unto me a broken heart and a contrite spirit. And whoso
cometh unto me with a broken heart and a contrite spirit, him
will I baptize with fire and with the Holy Ghost." (3 Nephi
9:20.)

I often wondered exactly what this meant. For years I could
not read the words "broken heart" without thinking of valen-
tines torn in half. Then I began to think that a broken heart
was one sorrowing for its sins. I still feel that this is part of it,
but there are so many passages where the Lord tells us to go in
peace, to lift up our heads, and so on. "What would the Lord

want with all those grieving hearts anyway?" I thought. Then I remembered watching my uncle breaking horses.

"THIS HORSE IS BROKEN"

One summer we rounded up some horses from the Nevada desert. There were some one- and two-year-old colts in the herd, and my uncle singled out two of them to break for riding. I was fascinated with his method of taming them.

First he roped them, then dragged them fighting and kicking into the chute corral. This corral narrowed at the end to barely the width of a horse's body. Here he could place a heavy leather halter over their heads without getting kicked. A thick rope was attached to the halter, and the end of the corral was opened. All of the boys would hang onto the rope while the horse reared and raced around the corral. We would half drag, half pull the colt to the center of the round corral, where a thick cedar post was set deep in the ground. Here we would cinch the rope, giving the horse about six to eight yards, and then back away.

The horses hated that rope. They would fight it for hours. Finally in exhaustion they would hang back on it, with their feet set firmly in the ground and all their weight pulling on the rope. Their eyes were wide, their tongues often hung out, and their ears were laid back. We watched them from the security of the corral fence.

In time, however, they learned that they only hurt themselves when they fought the rope. Then they approached the post, letting the rope hang slack. When this happened my uncle would slowly and gently walk closer. At first they would hang back again at his approach. If they did this, he would back away again. It didn't take long for the horses to learn that all they got by fighting was a stiff neck. Whenever I see the word *stiffneckedness* in the scriptures, I see those horses with their legs locked, hanging back on the rope.

In time my uncle could approach them and quietly calm them down. He would rub their sides and scratch them under their necks, all the while talking gently and lovingly. Soon he could uncinch the rope and teach them to follow his lead. When he could lay the rope across his open palm, turn his back on the horse, and walk with the horse following him, he would say, "This horse is broken."

A SUBMISSIVE, LOVING HEART

A broken heart is not a sorrowful heart mourning constantly over sin. It is a submissive heart, a trusting heart, a loving heart. It is a heart that says to the Savior, "Here is the rope of my life. Lay it across your palms that were wounded on Calvary. I will follow your lead. I will go wherever you wish to take me. I will not fight back." Why would any of us hesitate to go where the Savior would take us? Did He not promise to take us back into the presence of our Father in Heaven?

Our ability to survive the mists of mortality hinges to a great extent on our trust in and love of the Savior. We will do things out of love for Him that we might not do for anyone else. When Alma's own people were drifting into the mists of materialism and pride, he pulled them back by speaking of the Savior: "Behold, he sendeth an invitation unto all men, for the arms of mercy are extended towards them, and he saith: Repent, and I will receive you. Yea, he saith: Come unto me and ye shall partake of the fruit of the tree of life; yea, ye shall eat and drink of the bread and the waters of life freely. . . . And now I say unto you, all you that are desirous to follow the voice of the good shepherd, come ye out from the wicked, and be ye separate, and touch not their unclean things." (Alma 5:33–34, 57.)

LAKE ELIZABETH

I was teaching seminary in a small Latter-day Saint community many years ago. I noticed that many of the students were having problems as a result of the mists of the adversary. This was evident in their problems with dress, dating, music, and the Word of Wisdom. I was concerned and tried to teach lessons that would help the situation, but I did not feel I was having much success with a number of them. "How do I motivate them?" I frequently asked myself.

One night I had a dream that supplied an answer and changed my teaching emphasis from then on. I loved to backpack in Glacier National Park. There is a lake about ten miles into the backcountry called Elizabeth. It is a beautiful spot, with trees coming down the mountain slopes to the water's edge, and high peaks that are reflected on the calm surface of the lake. In the early morning you can smell the pines and hear the loons calling to each other as the mist rises from the lake surface. Of all the spots in creation, this one represents to me the earth's fullest measure of beauty.

In this dream I was walking along the path that leads to Lake Elizabeth. I had been on it many times and knew every bend in the trail. As I approached the lake, I heard loud voices. People were shouting and laughing, and piercing, hard music was playing. I quickened my pace and broke through the trees to the lakeshore. My eyes were greeted with a sight I never expected to see so far into the wilderness. Someone had cut down all the trees along the lake shore and in their place had erected tin huts on cement slabs. There was litter floating in the lake. The ground was polluted with all kinds of debris, and the smell of pine was replaced with a foul odor. Thousands of people were crowding the lake shore. They were all young and were engaged in all types of inappropriate behavior. Loud rock bands were playing in the tin sheds, and young couples were slipping off to be alone. There were drugs, alcohol, pornography, and foul language. Suddenly I began to recognize the faces of my students and soon picked out all 250 of them. Most of them were not directly involved in the activities along the lake shore but stood back, as if in doubt. I could see that they were tempted, pressured by others to join in the revelry, but something was holding them back from total surrender. A few had given in, however, and their surrender was making it even harder for the others to resist.

At this moment a finely dressed man stepped up to me. He was handsome and immaculately groomed. Every hair was in place. I could not tell how old he was, for he had an ageless quality about him, but his hair was silver gray. He was the handsomest man I had ever seen. He smiled with pleasure to see me and welcomed me to his world.

I was troubled by his manner and words but didn't know why. As soon as I could control myself, I asked him who he was and what had he done to my beautiful lake. He smiled again and said, "This is my church! These are my members! We are worshiping!" A scripture came to mind from the writings of Nephi: "Behold there are save two churches only; the one is the church of the Lamb of God, and the other is the church of the devil." (1 Nephi 14:10.)

I understood the symbolism of my dream. The pure, undefiled lake represented the world as the Father wanted it to be, but Satan and his followers were turning the world into a polluted, spiritual, moral waste that was destroying the noblest values of God's children.

As I understood the identity of my host, he remained quiet, studying me. When he saw that I recognized him for who he was, he smiled again. It gave him such pleasure to see the shocked and nervous expression on my face. This angered me somewhat. Mustering all my courage, I said to him, "These are my students, and you can't have them." At this announcement he smiled, confident in his power to hold them and eventually enslave and destroy them.

Finally he said, "Well, we'll see. In the meantime feel free to walk over my kingdom. Speak to your students. See if they will follow you out. See if there is anything in your scriptures or

COME OUT OF THE WORLD!

Church programs that is as exciting, gives as much pleasure, or is as inviting as the things I can offer them." He then turned and walked away as if I did not count for anything.

I rushed from student to student trying desperately to bring them out of the world with all of its false happiness. I spoke to each one, pleading, but when I was through I could gather only a small group. All during this desperate invitation, the silver-haired tempter stood quietly by, smiling. I could not convince the others to come out, and at this point I woke up.

This was a frustrating moment. I sensed that the dream was not over. I tried to go back to sleep to see its finish but found it impossible. I invented endings in my mind, but none of them seemed to fit. I lay awake in bed for a long time pondering and finally got up and went down to the seminary building. I couldn't get the dream out of my mind. I wanted to see its end.

While I reflected and pondered, the images returned, and the Lord finished it for me while I was awake. I returned to the lakeside. Everything was as before. I stood in the midst of my little group of students, wanting desperately to reach the rest but not knowing how or what to say. I asked the Lord, "What can I say that will cause them to respond? Teach me how to reach them." He answered my petition and gave me the words I would need. As loudly as I could, I called out the words: "*All those who love the Savior, come out of the world.*"

There was a moment of silence—everything stopped as if frozen in time. Then the heads of all the students I could not reach earlier turned and looked in the direction of the voice. It was as if a trumpet had called them to battle, and slowly but with determination, one by one, helping and encouraging one another, they came out of the world and gathered together. They came out not because of me, their parents, their bishops, or their friends. They came because they loved the Savior. They were His sheep, His sons and daughters, His beloved bride. In another world they had once followed Him over the great deceiver, and they would trust Him again.

There is great safety in the depth of our love for our Redeemer, Jesus Christ. I believe that the love of Christ can overcome the world. It will clear every mist along the path. It will strengthen us when we feel the pressure to surrender to the natural man.

"JESUS, THE VERY THOUGHT OF THEE"

"I would commend you to seek this Jesus of whom the prophets and apostles have written," Moroni wrote, "that the grace of God the Father, and also the Lord Jesus Christ, and the Holy Ghost, which beareth record of them, may be and abide in you forever." (Ether 12:41.) We must study the Savior's life, learn His words, and follow His example. Then our love for Him will be strong. We study the stories of Jesus and teach them to our families because they produce love for Christ. Thus the scriptures not only relate to us the commandments we must follow but also provide the chief motivating power to live them. If we know the commandments but cease to review the life of Christ, we remove a main source of motivation that makes obedience possible. Jesus himself said, "Learn of me, and listen to my words; walk in the meekness of my Spirit, and you shall have peace in me." (D&C 19:23.) We sing a hymn that says:

Jesus, the very thought of thee
With sweetness fills my breast;
But sweeter far thy face to see
And in thy presence rest.

Nor voice can sing, nor heart can frame,
Nor can the mem'ry find
A sweeter sound than thy blest name,
O Savior of mankind!

O hope of ev'ry contrite heart,
O joy of all the meek,
To those who fall, how kind thou art!
How good to those who seek!

Jesus, our only joy be thou,
As thou our prize wilt be;
Jesus, be thou our glory now,
And thru eternity.
(Hymns, *no. 141.*)

I believe in the power this hymn portrays. It was written in the 1100s, and its truth has blessed people now for almost a millennium. With our hearts full of love for the Master, we willingly, joyfully, and gratefully place the rope of our own agency into His hands and allow Him to lead us through every mist of darkness, around every snare, past every lie and deception, breaking every binding chain.

A DISTURBER AND AN ANNOYER

My ponderings that morning in my office did not end there. The students and I began to leave the lakeshore and disappear into the forest. The voices, music, and laughter began to fade. Suddenly one of the students, a senior boy who was an example of so much of the goodness of Latter-day Saint youth, tapped me on the shoulder and asked me to stop. The whole group stopped, and we listened to him. He turned back to the lake and pointed. "What about the rest of the people?" he said. "I can't leave them there, knowing whose power they are submitting to and what their eventual destiny will be. I'm going back to bring out as many as will listen to my voice."

All alone he walked back down the path to the lakeshore. Then a marvelous thing happened. One by one each of the students turned and followed him. They returned, not to join in the worldly activities but, trusting in the strength of Christ's

love for them and theirs for Him, to try to convince the rest of
God's children to seek all that is noble and virtuous in life.
They would teach them to love the Savior, and in that love to
abandon the pollutions of the world and walk in the purity of
the gospel.

One of my favorite statements of the Prophet Joseph Smith
is at the end of his account of the First Vision: "It seems as
though the adversary was aware, at a very early period of my
life, that I was destined to *prove a disturber and an annoyer of his
kingdom;* else why should the powers of darkness combine
against me?" (Joseph Smith—History 1:20.)

What was true of Joseph Smith is true of all of us. We were
born to disturb and annoy the devil's kingdom. His rule of the
lakeshore will not go unopposed. He will in the end be crushed,
just as the Lord indicated in the Garden of Eden before the
great battle began. We will be part of his defeat. We intend to
take possession of the entire earth, and we will do so. It should
not surprise us that he will hinder us at every turn, but the
Lord's "wisdom is greater than the cunning of the devil."
(3 Nephi 21:10.) Let us avail ourselves of that wisdom. It is
contained in the words of prophets and apostles, both written
and spoken. It is whispered by the Holy Ghost. It is exemplified
in the life of God's well-beloved Son. Let us trust in His love
for us and diligently labor to deepen our love for Him. Then, as
the Book of Mormon promises, we will "land [our] souls, yea,
[our] immortal souls, at the right hand of God in the kingdom
of heaven, to sit down with Abraham, and Isaac, and with
Jacob, and with all our holy fathers, *to go no more out.*"
(Helaman 3:30.) In that eternal kingdom, there are no mists of
darkness, and there are no shadows—only the pure light of
celestial glory.

KING BENJAMIN'S ADVICE

Once I went hiking in a canyon in southern Utah—a canyon that seemed to have no end. I was anxious to see the entire canyon and kept anticipating that with the next turn the end would come and I could retrace my steps, having completed the hike. But every new twist of the canyon brought a new vista of rock walls and boulders. I never did reach the end and still suspect that it goes on indefinitely.

When I began writing this book, I also thought it would have an end. I should have known that the scriptures are infinite in their applications and counsels. I wanted to unveil all of the tactics of the adversary, expose their weaknesses, and point out the defenses presented by the Lord. One of my main motivations was concern for my children and grandchildren and my desire to fortify my own will to resist. I finally had to admit that the theme I had chosen was too extensive. Sooner or later I would have to quit, just as I did that evening in the canyon. Ideas such as "Don't put barnwood on the temple" and "Sleeping through the Lord's alarm clock" would have to wait for another place and time.

With my realization, the words of King Benjamin rang truer

than ever before. He wanted to guard his people against the temptations they would face, but he knew that the task was too great for one person or one book. So I conclude with his conclusion and my testimony that every trap, snare, deception, lie, flattery, flaxen cord, pit, whirlwind, and fiery dart of the arch tempter is revealed in the scriptures. May we search them continually, for I am convinced that they hold the key to crushing his head in our own lives.

"And finally, I cannot tell you all the things whereby ye may commit sin; for there are divers ways and means, even so many that I cannot number them. But this much I can tell you, that if ye do not watch yourselves, and your thoughts, and your words, and your deeds, and observe the commandments of God, and continue in the faith of what ye have heard concerning the coming of our Lord, even unto the end of your lives, ye must perish. And now, O man, remember, and perish not." (Mosiah 4:29–30.)

INDEX